Christmas 2◊

Beth - What an
incredible journey this
has been with you!
Looks forward to a
lifetime of friendship
both at and away
from the barn. I
love you so much.
Thank you for all your
love + support.
Merry Christmas.
— Steffie

Riding into Your Mythic Life

Transformational Adventures with the Horse

PATRICIA BROERSMA

Foreword by Jean Houston

New World Library
Novato, California

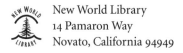

New World Library
14 Pamaron Way
Novato, California 94949

For permission acknowledgments, please see the Notes, which begin on page 195.

The material in this book is intended for education. It is not meant to take the place of diagnosis and treatment by a qualified medical practitioner or therapist. No expressed or implied guarantee as to the effects of the use of the recommendations can be given nor liability taken.

Text design by Tona Pearce Myers

Library of Congress Cataloging-in-Publication Data
Broersma, Patricia, 1946–
Riding into your mythic life : transformational adventures with the horse / Patricia Broersma ; foreword by Jean Houston.
    p.   cm.
Includes bibliographical references and index.
ISBN 978-1-57731-574-2 (hardcover : alk. paper)
1. Horsemanship—Therapeutic use. 2. Horses—Psychological aspects. 3. Human-animal relationships. I. Title.
RM931.H6B765 2007
615.8'515—dc22   2007030051

First printing, November 2007
ISBN-10: 1-57731-574-x
ISBN-13: 978-1-57731-574-2

Printed in Canada on acid-free, partially recycled paper

New World Library is a proud member of the Green Press Initiative.

10 9 8 7 6 5 4 3 2 1

For the horses who partner with us,
the people who dream a new world into being.

CONTENTS

Foreword by Jean Houston   ix

Preface   xiii

Introduction   1

1. THE POWER OF MYTH FOR YOUR LIFE
   Exploring a New Aspect of the Self   7

2. UNIVERSAL PATTERNS FOR YOUR
   LARGER LIFE PURPOSE
   Starring in Your Own Hero's Journey   17
   TRY THIS: Preparing for the Larger Journey with
        Adventure Games   36

3. HORSES FOR PARTNERSHIP AND
   NEW ADVENTURE
   Attuning Yourself to Subtle Communication   43
   TRY THIS: Lean on Me   57
   TRY THIS: Listening to Your Body   65

4. ALLIES FOR THE JOURNEY
Activating Aspects of the Self through Your Imaginal Body   71
TRY THIS: Developing Your Imaginal Body   76

5. ENERGY, COMMUNICATION,
AND THE EXPANDED SELF
Developing Tools for Healing   85
TRY THIS: Enhancing Your Touch   97

6. SYMBOLS TO SUSTAIN YOU ON THE JOURNEY
Reminding Yourself of Your Deeper Path   103
TRY THIS: Your Shield of Power   124

7. YOUR LIFE AS SACRED THEATER
Claiming Treasures through Ritual   129
TRY THIS: Journey Ride to Your Heart's Desire   143

8. MINDFULNESS IN EVERYDAY LIFE
Bringing Home Your Amplified Power   149
TRY THIS: Walking into Mindfulness   156

9. GLOBAL CITIZENSHIP
Bridging Multiple Worlds   159
TRY THIS: Widening Your World   174

Afterword: Dark Journey of the Green Horse   177
Acknowledgments   193
Notes   195
Index   201
About the Author   213

FOREWORD

SEVERAL YEARS AGO, I had the great pleasure to observe my friend and student Trish Broersma work with children with physical disabilities. Each child was placed on a horse and gently taught how to ride, but also how to do more than ride. The child learned how to interact with the horse, to join in heart and soul with this magnificent animal. Moving in rhythm with the horse, the child's body seemed to acquire something of the horse's natural splendor and sensitivity. Was it any wonder, then, that each child was thrilled, excited by new possibilities, new ways of being that gave them means beyond their physical limitations?

Broersma, whose attitude is always one of mythologizing rather than pathologizing, thus engages these children as little Centaurs, as the newest incarnation of the ancient partnership of human and horse. I am honored that she has incorporated some of my work in hers.

Watching her masterful teaching, I could only think how foolish we are to regard animals as inferior species — as our poor, if much loved, relations. And in that we are wrong. A man wise in the ways of animals, nature writer Henry Beston, once wrote:

> We need another and a wiser and perhaps a more mythical concept of animals. . . . We patronize them for their incompleteness, for their tragic fate of having taken form so far below ourselves. And therein we err, and greatly err. For the animal shall not be measured by man. In a world older and more complete than ours they moved finished and complete, gifted with extensions of the senses we have lost or never attained, living by voices we shall never hear. They are not brethren, they are not underlings; they are other nations, caught with ourselves in the net of life and time, fellow prisoners of the splendor and travail of the earth.

The mythical concept of animals and its relation to the horse is a theme of this remarkable book, and it informs the extraordinary nature of Broersma's innovative work. A lifelong devotee of the horse in all its capacities, this therapeutic riding instructor enters mythic domains that take her clients on journeys that heal as they transform. She understands the power and nature of myth as few others do.

What, after all, is myth? Myth is something that never was but is always happening. Myth is closer than breathing, nearer than our hands and feet; it is built into our very being. I have come to believe that life is allied with myth in order that we may advance along an evolutionary path. This path carries us nearer to the spiritual source, which lures us into even greater becoming. Myth is not a "no thing," an insubstantial, conceptual will-o'-the-wisp. It is coded into our cells, into the seas of the unconscious. It dwells in our little finger and plays along the spine as well as the spirit. It grants us access to the DNA of the human psyche, the source patterns originating in the ground of our being. It gives us the key to our personal and historical existence. Without mythic keys we would have neither culture nor religion, art, architecture, drama, ritual, social customs, or mental disorders. We would have only a gray world, with little if anything calling us forward to become all we can be.

Whenever I am teaching, I find that exploring a mythical or historical figure — someone who has through time and legend been rendered mythic within the context of a particular culture — allows people to see the experience of their own lives reflected in and ennobled by the story of that great life. Such work leads people into the discovery of their own larger story, for when actively pursued, myth leads us from the personal-particular concerns and frustrations of our everyday lives to the broader perspective of the personal-universal.

Working with myth, we assume the passion and the pathos of Isis as she seeks to recover the remains of her husband Osiris. We take on the quest for the Grail with Parsifal. We labor with Hercules and travel with Odysseus into the archetypal islands of inner and outer worlds. We explore new ways of peacemaking with Gandhi, learn the art of inventing society with Thomas Jefferson, and discover the basis for democracy with the Peacemaker, the creator of the Iroquois League. With the Persian mystic and teacher Rumi, we search for the soul's beloved. We join in sacred marriage and descend to the underworld with the great Sumerian goddess Inanna. Gradually we discover that these stories are our own stories, that they bear the amplified rhythms of our own lives.

When, like Trish Broersma, we bring the mythic journey to the most mythic of all creatures, the horse, we discover capacities we never knew we had. We have an intimate mythic companion in flesh and blood, a being of bounteous beauty and power who draws us into story, into adventure, into myth. We find connections to the greater natural world as well as an experience of subtle communication, one that can carry over to our dealings with other humans. We are sensitized, made more compassionate, and gifted with higher functioning.

What a delicious irony that being with horses in the ways that Trish Broersma teaches is an experience of becoming more fully human.

— Jean Houston, PhD

PREFACE

BY THE TIME MY THIRD HORSE, Violet Emerald, arrived, I had ridden hundreds of horses and had no idea that she would usher in a whole new way of life, not only for me but also for others. I only knew that her dark eyes and something indefinable about her called to me from a mere snapshot. Her unusually feminine name hinted of the future, but it would be years before I claimed the promise of that name. Not realizing it at the time, I was on the brink of a mythic journey that would redefine my understanding of partnership and power, and call me to new inner and outer terrain.

Not long before Emerald's arrival, I had spent about twelve years focused on activities that had little to do with horses — graduate school, marriage, and my three children. During this time, I rarely saw a horse except on an occasional vacation trail ride with a rented horse. Riding those horses, which were usually ill-mannered, burned out, and underfed, I longed to return to the intimacy and adventure I had known with horses in my younger years, when I had ridden and taught. I would sometimes gaze across an open field, breathing deeply of the fresh country air that was in short supply in my urban neighborhood. I recalled the pungent, earthy smell of a horse's hide, the sweet fragrance of fresh-mown hay, the alfalfa-green breath of a grazing horse as he raised his head to blow a greeting. My body remembered the complex rhythms of solitary rides when I dared to sing freely and slightly out of tune. I recalled races across arenas and fields, and horse shows when I competed to win that astonishing first blue ribbon, and summer camps where I gave youngsters their first taste of adventure on horseback.

My first childhood love had been horses, but beginning in college, following my heart increasingly meant offering service to humankind in bigger ways than seemed possible in the world of horses. After graduate school I married and soon became pregnant with our first son, Matthew. That first childbirth was a revelation: I felt that I had experienced a miracle. My husband and I built a partnership that had us both changing diapers and cooking meals, enjoying common interests, and supporting each other's work in the world, which, for me, was community development and freelance graphic design.

After the birth of two more children, my husband and I concluded it was time for me to step back into the world of horses. I visited a nearby horse trainer who operated out of a large stable where people boarded horses or rented ones to ride through the nearby park. Before long, I assisted in the training of most of his clients' horses and his riding students, and accompanied them to horse shows. I gloried in horses again, fitting in a few hours whenever the children were in school and I could break away from my graphic design business.

The trainer I worked for (whom I'll call Terry) had built his reputation by taking horses that other trainers would not or could not work with, often because of intractable behavior problems. Owners wanted him to prepare their horses for the show ring. This was a familiar world to me from my teen and college years. The horses were mostly American Saddlebreds, a hot breed noted for glamorous, high energy when charging around a show ring. Terry was like that too. His charisma attracted riding students as well as training clients. His smiling extroversion provided a happy, safe place for people, especially youngsters, to play out their fascination with horses. The warm winters of San Antonio, Texas, encouraged year-round riding. Terry was successful with the horses he trained, marked by his consistently placing in the top five ribbons in horse show classes.

As I became more acquainted with Terry's training methods, however, I began to question them. On the one hand, he provided an opportunity for horses and riders to come together, embraced by his sunny disposition. Weekends and afternoons were crowded at the stable, with women, a few men, and teens hanging out with their horses, taking lessons, and riding nearby trails. I gained valuable experience in being assertive and sensitive with equally assertive and sensitive horses. Other times, however, when just Terry and I were working, things were different. He would return to the barn from a training ride with a lathered, hot, tired horse that had a blood-flecked, foaming mouth or a gouged chin from the action of the curb chain on a long-shank bit. Other times the horse would have a blood-striped flank from the whip. Initially wishing to avoid leaping to conclusions without more information, I watched and inquired. Terry explained that he had to "get the horse's attention" to give the clients what they wanted and to give the horse any kind of viable future.

I wanted to believe in his approach, but I needed more information to do so. I began to realize that, along with his charm and ability with horses, Terry occasionally unleashed his anger on a horse. One time, for instance, he was grooming his Shetland pony, who accompanied him as a trick pony in a variety of venues. Terry leaned over the pony's head from the front to adjust his mane just behind the ears. The pony tossed his head, knocking Terry in the jaw. Terry raised his fist and punched the pony so hard on the side of the head that the pony fell to the ground. I knew that standard safety procedure warned against standing where Terry had stood with the pony, precisely because of this kind of risk, and I was stunned that he had responded as though the pony had attacked him, when in fact the pony could just as easily have reacted to a fly or some other distraction. When I challenged Terry, he said that the pony should have known better. I had my doubts. Terry's response seemed unwarranted and extreme. I began to seriously question his training methods, although, at the time, I had little inkling of where that questioning would lead.

One day Terry unleashed his anger on me. I was preparing to go into the show ring on one of the horses that I had trained for one of his clients. A rider in the previous class had borrowed my gloves and bridle, so I worked quickly to bridle my horse and then wrestled with the tight leather gloves to pull them onto my sweaty hands in the summer heat. I felt anxious and vulnerable because I wanted to perform well for the trainer, as well as for the horse and his owner since it was this horse's first show. Terry approached me and, to my astonishment, instead of helping me prepare, berated me for delaying the class, demanding, "Who do you think you are, making everyone wait on you? Hurry up!" He didn't seem to hear my explanation that I had made advance arrangements with the show manager for the delay. His barrage continued until I finally mounted and headed into the ring. I mentally shut off the whole incident, knowing that I needed to focus on the horse for the next twenty minutes of show time. Inwardly, though, I was devastated and knew that I could not let this incident pass. After the class, I confronted him, but he claimed he did not even recall the incident. Knowing I was speaking in the swell of emotion, I waited until the next day to approach him again for more discussion. He still did not recall the incident, and his sincerity was convincing.

The strangeness of his forgetfulness did not get my attention as much as his anger. I realized that most people accepted male anger as typical or routine, and what I had experienced with Terry was similar to what I had witnessed in his treatment of some of the horses. From a fresh perspective, I saw that power over a horse was condoned and expected in order to elicit the best performance. Occasionally that power was wielded in the heat of emotion.

To Terry's credit, he asked me to warn him whenever I saw him acting angrily toward a horse. He knew that his behavior was inappropriate. But as time passed I realized that we were dealing with a larger, more complex matter than Terry's personal issues. The situation had its roots in a culture that expected horses to work to meet the man-made standards of the show ring, a culture that was accustomed to asserting power with little consideration of others' perspectives, whether of horses or people.

Finally, even though I was aggrieved to turn my back on the horses and riders, I knew that I had to stop working with Terry. At a gut level I knew that I was up against a situation that was outmoded in some fundamental way, even though I loved many aspects of it, including the people and the horses. It was a matter of my being true to what I knew was right: to honor myself and the horses. Only later did I realize that I was being forced to forge a more conscious relationship to partnership and power that would have far-reaching implications. I was entering a mythic story that mirrored the larger pattern of the times I lived in.

After several months, the owners of the stable where I had worked with Terry asked me to take charge of their own teaching program. Hoping I could somehow create a better situation for us all, I was happy to return to my horse and human friends in a new context. At the same time, my husband suggested that I purchase my own horse, a delightful prospect that I had deemed impossible because of our family responsibilities, especially since my husband shared little interest in horses.

During this time I traveled to Oklahoma City and visited some friends who had a large Arabian training operation. There, a friend handed me a photograph of a horse in Kentucky that was for sale. The three-year-old Saddlebred mare was already in foal and due to deliver the next spring. Her name, Violet Emerald, was not a traditional Saddlebred name, which is usually something bold and European sounding such as King, Bourbon, Peabody, or Shamrock. By contrast, hers seemed feminine and flowery, and because I was still aligned to the tradition of masculine ways in this world of horses, it would not appeal to me for months. But the dark eyes I saw in the snapshot spoke to something deeper than these issues. They called to me from the place of mystery that had been seeded years ago with the birth of my first child, and no doubt even before that.

I put in a phone call. The owner's first comment about Emerald was that she had the boldest, prettiest eyes she had ever seen on a Saddlebred. I was hooked, and the practicalities worked themselves out. By fall of that year, Violet Emerald arrived after an easy two-day transport from Kentucky. When she stepped carefully out of the van, her long, black mane and tail were unkempt but elegant. The driver of the horse transport reported that she was one of the quietest horses he'd handled, considering she was only three years old. I happily held her lead rope and gratefully took this new presence into my life, sensing even then, however dimly, the high promise of the future story before us. With dark, wide eyes, she raised her head high and snorted her greeting to all about her. A few weeks later, thinking perhaps I was disappointed that Emerald didn't trot out in the high spirits of a show horse, Terry predicted — accurately, it would turn out — that I would come to treasure Emerald's calm nature.

In the years that followed, it was the dark mystery of those eyes and the unorthodox, yet increasingly appropriate, nature of her name that helped to guide me on my own unorthodox path into a new relationship between horses and humans. I moved to a larger stable and began training horses and teaching riding, ultimately creating the largest youth riding program in San Antonio at that time.

I began to incorporate my interest in literature and other cultures into my work with riders and horses. I developed an adventure camp for my advanced riding students where, on horseback, we acted out myths from a variety of cultures. We became knights on a quest for the Holy Grail in an elaborate trail ride/treasure hunt. We painted our horses with Native American symbols and rode bareback on an imaginary journey around the medicine wheel of life. We enacted some of Hanuman's adventures in the *Ramayana*, a Hindu epic. This surely was a considerable departure from the traditional riding program, but it whetted my taste for creating something new for my students.

At about the same time, I stumbled onto the field of therapeutic horseback riding when I read a newspaper article about a program in San Antonio. The idea that horseback riding could actually be a healing modality for children with disabilities began to grow in my mind. I had already known its power over the lives of some of my students. For instance, one young girl had been suicidal during her parents' divorce. Years later they told me that riding had saved her life. In another instance, a fourth-grade boy was a bit clumsy and bumped into things at the stable. It wasn't until he had ridden with me for more than a year that I learned from his mother that, prior to starting riding, he had not known how to read. We had been unaware of his learning disabilities. The mother had not connected riding and reading until a year later, when she noticed that his reading reached a plateau whenever he took a break from riding, but improved once his riding lessons began again. I was fascinated by the connection of rhythmic movement with brain functioning.

I knew that I wanted to find a way to bring horses to others like these students, so that they, too, could benefit. Because it was based on a profit-making model, the horse show industry did not encourage such endeavors. That model no longer compelled me. My heart led me in a new direction, one that combined an earlier interest in medicine with my interest in horses. My knowledge that Emerald's greatest talents did not lie in the competitive horse-show world supported me in this direction also.

Though she competed successfully, winning top ribbons in the Country Pleasure division at local horse shows, what Emerald excelled at was welcoming a new rider. Her calm demeanor inspired trust from beginning riders. At the same time, she challenged them to give her clear and assertive signals when they wanted a livelier ride. She stood quietly for a young rider's stumbling efforts to groom and tack her up for a lesson. She lowered her head and blew gently into the face of a new and timid young student. Looking back, I see that both Emerald and I were headed for something different from tradition's previous dictates.

After completing undergraduate requirements for medical school, I had turned away from pursuing medicine in the face of the distasteful competitive atmosphere of the premedical courses. However, my interest in medicine and healing arts began to reemerge as I explored the possibility that I could combine them with horses in the field of therapeutic riding. Within a few months I began to incorporate mildly disabled students into my riding program, and I joined the North American Riding for the Handicapped Association (NARHA). Before long, I established a second nonprofit program for therapeutic riding in San Antonio, a city large enough to support several such programs.

Shortly after getting that program accredited with NARHA, in 1992 I moved to the Rogue Valley of southern Oregon, where I directed a similar program for nine years. There, one of our board members encouraged us to offer a program for at-risk teens in our local residential treatment center. Chris Duke had known horses as a life-saving part of his own teen years that had enabled him to leave behind the drugs and alcohol that had ruined his life. Now he wanted to offer this solution to other at-risk teens. I realized that I could adapt the Adventure Camp program I had offered in San Antonio to these basically able-bodied students. They could easily participate in the activities that had been a part of that program. Over the next seven years, the initial ten-week program for young women was expanded to a similar program for young men and adults.

I carried into these newer programs the basic principles for the Adventure Camp I had developed previously in San Antonio: myth and the horse–human connection were explored for developing compassion, partnership, and sensitive communication. These skills helped build global citizenship and engender the understanding that we each embark upon a "hero's journey" when we embrace the mythic proportions of our own lives. Residential treatment center staff accompanying clients to our program often said they found the work as life-changing for themselves as it was for their clients. They enthusiastically supported the program as an effective enhancement of their treatment program. It was not a therapy experience, but an enriched experiential educational program centering around the same principles as the treatment center's therapy, only from a fresh, unique perspective.

I soon realized that I could bring those same benefits back to my seriously disabled students, who were just as eager for their own adventures of body, mind, and spirit. Even our riders with profound autism and severe disabilities insisted on adventure games and accomplished feats that amazed parents and staff.

Within just a few years, my riding instruction and horse training had verged away from tradition to begin focusing on how riding could bring unparalleled benefits to people with issues as widely varied as head injuries, learning disabilities, and autism. Along with other horses, Emerald took my students and me into explorations of different ways of being in the world, gleaned from understanding other cultures and exploring our own inner frontiers. My story echoed the broader journey of our global human community, striving to move away from debilitating conflict toward more effective forms of partnership and power. Along the way, I had grown into a new way of being a woman in a man's world, through learning new ways to bridge all kinds of differences. I gained tools for learning and teaching the arts of compassion and insight, intuition and discernment, body-based knowing, and energy medicine.

In sharing this work at various professional conferences, I was repeatedly encouraged to expand it into a book so that others could take their own mythic journeys with their horse companions. For horse enthusiasts, trainers, educators, therapists, and anyone seeking positive change in their lives, this book invites everyone to claim the grand adventure of their own lives.

INTRODUCTION

EVERYONE WHO HAS ADMIRED A HORSE galloping across a field or experienced the beauty of a horse such as Shadowfax in *The Lord of the Rings* films has stepped into his or her mythic life, if only for a moment. These individuals have had a taste of the intimate relationship between horses and humans that has spanned centuries and populated one great story after another, entertaining, teaching, and inspiring us. Because of this rich heritage that has bound our lives to theirs, by their very nature, horses are mythic creatures. They have become associated in our collective imagination with aspects of the human journey at its greatest. By learning through this book how to take advantage of these special moments that horses offer, you can take a journey on an unparalleled path of spiritual transformation, opening the way for your own human journey at its greatest.

This book offers horse enthusiasts and professionals, mental health professionals, and educators experiential opportunities for exploring and expanding their human potential in the areas of mind, body, and spirit through powerful experiences with horses. These experiences teach skills for developing intuition, compassion, and leadership; and for stepping into one's greater life. They give ways to explore oneself as an energetic being and to develop the ability to communicate with others more skillfully. They help cultivate an awareness of subtle cues in oneself and others, including horses, and ways to orchestrate this awareness for a more joyful and effective life. They nurture skills for global citizenship, promoting cross-cultural interaction in our increasingly complex world.

The power of the horse to change people's lives was recognized decades ago with the birth of the field of therapeutic riding. Early practitioners of therapeutic riding in Europe began to formalize the field in the 1940s, and from there it migrated to the United States. In those early years, therapeutic riding was considered either a form of physical therapy conducted by those licensed for that purpose, or a form of recreation for disabled people conducted by riding instructors. In 1969 the North American Riding for the Handicapped Association (NARHA) was formed to bring standards of professionalism and safety to the field and provide a forum for collegial networking. By the 1980s, programs were offered in most of the major cities in the United States. Most of those programs were run by nonprofit organizations affiliated with horse facilities that offered traditional horse training and riding lessons.

During that time, therapeutic riding programs focused on bringing a better quality of life to people in wheelchairs, children with developmental delays, and others with a wide range of disabilities. People who had never dreamed that they could be outdoors on a horse were offered inspiring and empowering opportunities for exercise and recreation; many of them experienced a kind of mobility that previously was out of reach.

This growth of therapeutic riding programs paralleled a nation-wide trend to include people with disabilities in the mainstream population. No longer were they tucked away in institutions, hidden from the eyes of others. Instead, people everywhere were finding ways to keep their hearts and communities open to *all* their fellow citizens. Schools began to have more-effective special-education programs, and many of the students in those programs began to have access to therapeutic riding programs as one of their weekly activities. Parents seeking all kinds of benefits for their children with special needs were thrilled to see them blooming physically, mentally, and psychologically on the back of a horse. For these children, the day they got to ride a horse was the highlight of their week. Noting the remarkable benefits of riding for their clients, pioneering therapists incorporated riding into physical, occupational, and speech therapies.

Reflecting increasing interest in the mental health aspects of therapeutic riding, in 1996 the Equine Facilitated Mental Health Association (EFMHA) was formed as a special-interest section of NARHA. It attracted those trained in counseling and psychotherapy, but also riding instructors who wished to attend to broader issues of human development for their students. EFMHA members, unlike most others in NARHA, were outspoken about the sentient nature of the horse and the spiritual and emotional benefits that paralleled other, more tangible, physical benefits.

More recently, in the past five years, EFMHA has experienced dramatic growth as special-education professionals, coaches, psychotherapists, and others have begun to offer experiences with horses in all kinds of venues as a vital part of their lessons or sessions. Corporations send groups to work with leadership coaches and horses for workplace team building and problem solving. Special-education teachers bring entire classrooms to the barn for full curricula in reading, math, and other skills that can be associated with the riding lesson.

The number of programs in therapeutic riding has grown so that nearly every community in the United States offers a program of some sort, though they vary widely in size and services offered. The horses in this work are increasingly recognized as equal partners in the therapeutic team, rather than primarily a tool used for therapeutic benefits to the rider. EFMHA recently developed training for horse professionals who wish to work with educators and therapists in a three-part team composed of the horse, the equine specialist, and the educator or therapist. This training and other efforts of EFMHA are shifting the paradigm from using horses as a tool for human ends to enlisting the horse as a sentient, capable team member in teaching situations. Their work is part of the broader emergence of the feminine in our world, which reaches for a balance with the predominantly masculine history of the past several-thousand years.

This book is part of that paradigm shift. Based in this most recent stage in the evolution of the horse–human relationship, it treats horses as teachers of sensitive communication, as sentient beings who can give us a new perspective on our world, our own lives, and the potential for working in cooperative partnerships for world-changing situations.

What activates all the experiences in this book, making them more profoundly transformational, is the framework of myth as a foundational aspect of the self, where we find that we can live our lives in much grander scale, with more companions than we dreamed possible. Horses provide a natural and powerful vehicle for entering this mythic aspect of the self. They have an irresistible allure for most people, a mysterious attraction, based on a profound connection that reaches into human prehistory and deeply into the human psyche.

Human cultures all over the world have relied on the horse for transportation and draft power for thousands of years. From the ancient Bronze Age civilizations in China, India, and the Middle East to the pastoral peoples of the Asian Steppe and the native peoples of the North American plains, horses have been an inescapable part of daily life and culture. Enshrined in religious belief, cosmology, and mythology, they have played an important role in shaping how people make sense of the world. Today the utilitarian value of the horse has been almost completely replaced by the automobile, tractor, and truck, but horses can still have considerable influence in our lives. Indeed, the symbolic power of the horse is all the more significant now that horses have mostly shed their practical roles in human societies. Horses are free to exert their influence on our imaginations, to exist for us as mythic creatures that can elicit our own mythic selves.

This book draws on the symbolically rich, mythic aspect of horses rooted in millennia of human history. It invites you to explore the events of your life as a mythic adventure, a hero's journey in which you, mounted on a horse — both metaphorically and physically — star in the leading role.

While other books emphasize primarily the healing aspects of work with horses, or discuss mythology in a theoretical manner, this book focuses on practically exploring myth and partnership with horses, recognizing the larger patterns of one's life, and developing human skills that bring celebration, empowerment, and greater joyfulness. This approach enables you to reframe your life into a much larger context through activities with myth and horses, allowing for even painful events to contribute to moving ahead in your life with renewed commitment and enthusiasm.

This work brings us back to our vital connection with the natural world and encourages us to act in groups with a modus operandi of cooperation instead of competition. To take on the challenge of preserving our planet, we must find ways to cooperate with those who are vastly different from ourselves. Those others are not just peoples from bewilderingly different cultures, but creatures of other species as well. Many horses have consented to help us in this endeavor.

CHAPTER ONE

THE POWER OF MYTH
FOR YOUR LIFE

Exploring a New Aspect of the Self

THERE'S NOTHING BETTER FOR THE SOUL than a good story. The stories that have been retold over and over hold power over our imaginations. Horses are often present in these stories, carrying a hero or heroine in grand style, galloping across a faraway beach like the Black Stallion and the boy Alec, or rearing like the Lone Ranger and Silver in the landscapes of the American West. Horses lend their qualities of physical power, dramatic movement, and beauty, extending the actions of characters beyond human limitations. In doing so, they enhance the soul-charging power of a good story. The power of those stories also relies on the underlying patterns that call us to attention and teach us about the important fundamentals of life. These are the enduring stories that beg to be given new form, generation after generation — the stories that started around a campfire and were repeated by traveling actors or the tribe's gifted storyteller, who

7

enhanced old stories with song, dance, and drama to help the community face particular challenges. Centuries later such powerful stories took written form in books, then visual form with television and movies.

Jean Houston's pioneering work in human development illuminates the power of story by structuring the human self in four levels. The third level is the mythic/symbolic aspect of the self, which is the realm of story, the level we will focus on. This does not mean that we will ignore the first two levels: the physical/sensory aspect, which has to do with such personal characteristics as the color of our hair and how we perceive the world around us; and the second, psychological/historical aspect of the self, which has to do with our personality patterns and personal history. Nor will we sidestep the fourth level, which is the spiritual or unitive aspect of the self in which we realize union with all of life. We will find that if we delve deeply into any one of these realms, as in this book, where we will focus on the mythic, we will activate all the others. For example, an intensely physical experience, such as sports competition, can trigger experiences on the other levels of the self: psychological, mythic, and spiritual.

Understanding Houston's concept of the self helps to open our understanding of the potency of the mythic aspect of the self. It is far more than an elaboration of psychological patterns that give insight into our behavior. Rather, when this rich realm is explored, doors open to remarkable, even miraculous, adventures in our own lives. This is the realm where great stories come alive within us. We have our own adventures, tragedies, and comedies. When we have a heightened sense of the power of this mythic realm, we can step forth on our journey with new vigor, traveling farther and deeper than we ever dreamed possible. We can step into the starring role in the play of our own lives, with a cast of thousands supporting us, and know that we are part of everyone else's supporting cast as well.

In the mythic realm, a visual image or story points to less-visible realities in our lives and world. When we explore the mythic aspect of our lives, we find that our psychology is blown open into something much greater, and that we are more than complex mechanisms of flesh and blood at the mercy of our egos, driven to and fro by the melodramas of our emotional lives. We discover an enlarged sense of purpose for our lives, playing the lead role in our own sacred drama. We are put in touch with a higher part of ourselves. Jean Houston describes the higher self this way: "Beyond the surface and literal there seems to lie the self's larger vision and comprehension of itself. This larger vision makes itself known as an entelechy, a higher version of the self, a dynamic purposiveness and full capacity of a person that is contained almost as an autonomous self within the self."[1]

By their very nature, horses are mythic creatures that invite us to step into that higher sense of purpose for our lives, to become better acquainted with our entelechy. Just by being in the horse's presence and making the horse one player in our cast of thousands, we can ride into this potent realm of story and myth. In our imaginations, horses are typically associated with extraordinary beauty, movement, and power. For that reason, our association with them gives us the opportunity to plumb the mythic aspects of ourselves that lie just beneath the surface of consciousness.

Consider the poem "The Myth: Raison d'Être" by Pattiann Rogers:

Some say there are wild white ponies
Being washed clean in a clear pool
Beneath a narrow falls in the middle
Of the deciduous forest existing
At the center of the sun.

Some say the thrashing of those ponies
Straining against their bridles, the water flying
From their stamping hooves in fiery pieces
And streaks rising higher than the sandbar willows

Along the bank, drops whirling like sparks
From the manes of their shaking heads,
And the shouting and splashing of the boys
Yanked off their feet by the ponies

As they attempt to wash the great shoulders
And rumps of those rearing beasts, as they lather
Their necks and breasts, stroking them,
Soothing them — all this is the source
Of the fierce binding and releasing energy
Existing at the core of the sun.

The purple jays, mad with the chaos,
Shrieking in the tops of the planetrees,
The rough-winged swallows swerving back
And forth in distress, the struggle of the boys
To soap the inner haunch, to reach
Beneath the belly, to dodge the sharp
Pawing hooves, the wide-eyed screaming

Of the slipping ponies being maneuvered
For the final rinse under the splattering falls —
All the fury of this frightening drama,
Some believe, is contained and borne steadily
Across the blue sky strictly by the startling
Light and combustion of its own commotion.

But when those ponies stand, finally quiet,
Their pure white manes and tails braided
With lilac and rock rose, the boys asleep
On their backs, when they stand,
Fragrant and shimmering, their forelocks
Damp with sweet oil, serene and silent
In the motionless dark of the deep
Riverside forest, then everyone can
Easily see and understand the magnificent
Silhouette, the restrained power, the adorned,
Unblemished and abiding beauty
That is the night.[2]

Imagine taking the images of this poem with you into your day. Think of translating it into your own daily tasks, such as corralling a houseful of young children through a weekend's activities, keeping the attention of a classroom of teenagers, or directing a staff meeting of employees in a growing company. Your own experience with a horse can intensify this poem's vivid imagery even more, and your day's encounters with chaos may become "... the source / Of the fierce binding and releasing energy..." at the center of your life. When you come to the end of a day, a project, or an effort, perhaps you will rest and reflect, sleep as do the boys, with a kind of redeeming benediction as you refresh yourself with the thought that "... everyone can / Easily see and understand the magnificent / Silhouette, the restrained power, the adorned, / Unblemished and abiding beauty / That is the night."

Or you might read the mythic tale of Bellerophon's powerful partnership with Pegasus, which gave Bellerophon the ability to win such unusual challenges as the defeat of the horrible Chimera. It is a story with a cautionary warning of the consequences of exploiting power: When he flew too near Mt. Olympus and was tossed back to earth, Bellerophon became crippled for life. When this story is heard with enough accompanying drama, poetry, and beauty, it awakens another part of oneself. If you take that experience into the real-life situation of learning to ride in harmony with a horse, it may evoke your own power for that and other situations. For example, you may step into your work life with a clearer understanding of how to create effective partnerships in the business world based on mastering the complexities of communication with your horse — with a healthy dose of reality-checking for your limitations.

When you allow a story to interact with your own life in this way, you experience a bit of the power of myth, and you become more acquainted with your own mythic life. In the world of psychotherapy, personality patterns are sometimes given the enlightening names of classical gods. For instance, Artemis gives form to the kind of personality that is the virginal woman of nature and the wilds, as opposed to Aphrodite, whose talents lie in her relationships with men. *Women Who Run with the Wolves*, by Clarissa Pinkola Estés, and other works have beautifully elaborated these archetypal patterns to provide means of gaining insight into the psychological patterns ruling one's life. However, when we understand through working with horses that the mythic realm goes beyond the psychological realm, we find that we are dealing with our connection to larger patterns of reality, to a kind of energetic network that connects all living beings.

Becoming more conscious of this mythic realm allows us to access parts of ourselves that usually lie dormant. This reaches far beyond any mental configurations of one's personality patterns and way of being in the world. However subtle or hidden, the mythic realm is a real aspect of our lives. We can enter into a real and dynamic relationship with a larger life that responds to, and is molded by, our interaction with it. For instance, when we explore the psychological archetype of Athena, we can shed light on personality patterns that lead some to become leaders and caretakers of their communities, as Athena did in the ancient Greek world. A woman with a personality aligned with the archetype of Athena will tend to take leadership positions in which she supports large, overarching programs. Instead of pursuing romantic involvement, she will tend to invest herself as a powerful friend to those making heroic efforts. She will have a broad view for the well-being of the community and far-sightedness to perceive its future needs.

We can enter into a more vital relationship with archetypes such as these when we understand that there is a mythic dimension to our own lives. We can enter the mythic realm with an archetype such as Athena as more than an abstract pattern. She can become a vital, mythic companion, offering us opportunities to interact and actually grow with the archetype as we, together with it, take on new evolutionary forms. Athena, who was born from the head of her father and so adopted a masculine style of leadership, may need new chapters of her story for our time, wherein she finds a source for her missed mothering and develops new ways of leadership that embrace that newly awakened feminine aspect of herself.

Perhaps the Statue of Liberty stands as one manifestation for this dynamic of Athena's evolving form. Lady Liberty is an evolved Athena because she has grown with times that needed an inspiring figure to welcome immigrants to our country. Because her story is essentially created in the context of our own mythic story, as we develop more-embracing ways of leadership, we can feel accompanied by more than just our flesh and blood selves. As we explore new forms of leadership that rely on some of our more feminine aspects, men and women alike, we find that we are larger than just our own day-to-day individual lives. We are part of the large imaginal world that is our mythic life.

Myth gives our lives extended avenues of adventure. We acquire frameworks for setting forth with courage into new directions, with a sense of purpose and destiny strengthening us. Horses occupy that land where myth opens the door to our greater lives. When we understand that myth is not just some fictional version of real life, but a dynamic and rich adventure waiting to be lived, then horses can become our steeds for riding into that life. When we become more aware of the potency of the mythic dimension, we find that our former problems, neuroses, or illnesses are transformed. Instead of problems, they become juicy parts of our mythic lives, challenges that make our lives interesting, and frameworks for our life journeys. Our hang-ups, warts, mistakes, and embarrassing secrets are returned to us as a dramatic piece of live theater in which we star and also provide supporting roles for others' starring roles. Instead of being caught in a psychological framework that often lends pathological labels to our eccentricities, we can live our own grand lives in mythic proportions.

We find that the community we live in is made up of more than human beings and creatures of flesh and blood. It is populated by beings who dwell also in the land of myth. We can choose to interact with that wider world that they and we inhabit together. This is the adventure that this book invites you to explore.

Our own adventures are nested within the larger mythic patterns of our times. It is interesting and important to explore new myths emerging now, for we are creators of those myths, whether we realize it or not. Our recent cultural experience has been grounded primarily in the breakup of past myths that gave purpose and meaning to people's lives. For decades, established patterns in church, family, and community — what was once considered right beyond doubt — have been dissolving. The national patriotism appropriate for earlier world wars is now challenged by those who insist on a global patriotism in situations of conflict. Hundreds of thousands of people anchor their spiritual lives in practices based on various religious traditions rather than one true way. In the face of this radical change, others dig into their traditions of the past with fundamentalist passion. Unprecedented violence populates our media in both fictional and factual stories. In the face of crumbling myths, something new is forming, like a phoenix rising from its ashes.

We have critical choices before us that determine the character of the future myth. Because we are so immersed in the process, it is challenging to see the broader mythic patterns emerging. It is easy to be paralyzed to inaction by the overwhelming nature of current affairs, or to rant against the people we consider responsible. Living our mythic lives to their fullest potential in the midst of our times means we must deepen into our own selves for an approach that can harness the necessary passion for something new that we can celebrate, forging dynamic new ways of being that embrace the complexity of our world. That is the moral imperative of a new myth for the future.

When I speculate on the nature of current and future myth, I enjoy exploring how this new myth is being given form by the Internet and email communications. With the massive numbers of emails that connect us with people all over the world relatively easily compared to ten years ago, we are building a more and more tangible network of connection among human communities. I imagine it as a web of strands of light, given energy by our messages to one another, laying down the fundamentals of an underlying pattern that will eventually grow into a significant force in the world as it reaches critical mass. It is an element of the myth that is emerging for our own times, a modern form of the Hindu Indra's net that extended out from the palace of the god on Mount Meru, with jewels at the junction of each strand of the net, each reflecting all the other jewels and demonstrating our infinite mutual relations with one another.

Working with horses is aligned with this same evolutionary trend, building connections between species the way the Internet builds connections of another sort. Horses' mythic role in human life evolves into something new as we embark with them on our own adventures. Horses can usher us into the greater adventure of our lives in any number of ways. For instance, when horses are not emotionally shut down by abuse, they are master teachers of subtle communication, responding to delicate cues from humans that emanate from our emotional states and patterns held from our life experiences. Horses notice these things and respond to them. When we decide to enter into communication with them at this level, they can be remarkable partners in building the web that connects us all.

The mythic aspect of the self is obviously rich with story. In fact this aspect of the self can be liberated by participation in symbolic dramas in which it emerges clothed in mythic form. When allied with our own lives, a good story of mythic proportions becomes a potent vehicle for becoming conscious of our highest calling — our entelechy — for discerning our purpose in life, and for connecting us to new levels of energy within and without ourselves. We find that our own stories become manifest in mythic proportions, making our lives larger than we had previously dared dream, with the horse a large-hearted and powerful character in that story.

CHAPTER TWO

UNIVERSAL PATTERNS FOR
YOUR LARGER LIFE PURPOSE

Starring in Your Own Hero's Journey

JOSEPH CAMPBELL GATHERED THOUSANDS OF MYTHS during his lifetime and discerned a common pattern, which he called the hero's journey. Myth after myth, story after story, legend after legend told the tale of an often ordinary character whose daily life is interrupted by a call to adventure, whether through a charge from the gods in ancient Greece, the yearning of a girl named Cinderella to attend a ball, a ring discovered by a humble Hobbit, or a message from Hogwarts for a boy named Harry Potter. By a variety of adventures, the hero or heroine is transported from an old way of being, gaining new skills and insights and finally bringing those benefits back home.

Jean Houston talks about how this applies to our own lives in this way: "Everyone's life changes in its accoutrements — clothing styles change, jobs are created that were once never heard of, new cars and all kinds of new things surround us — but there are universal elements that do not: movement out of an outmoded condition into a larger experience of amplified power, where we find new sources, new greening. After having profound initiations, we find potentials we didn't know we had, find new sources of strength, renewal, and we bring them back to our everyday life."[1] This is the mythic aspect of your life and mine, our own hero's journey. The best, most universal stories and movies, for instance, the *Harry Potter* books and films, *The Lord of the Rings*, *The Black Stallion*, and the *Star Wars* trilogy, are structured on these fundamental themes. They are there in the stories of Ulysses and other ancient heroes. They are told and retold because of their evocative power for our own lives.

There are a number of stages in the classical hero's journey that are universal to us all. The journey begins with a call to adventure that often is refused initially. Allies show up to help, and the hero finally assents to the journey ahead and sets out on a quest that often enters into a new landscape. At the outset, there is a test of some sort, such as a dragon at the door, which the hero must defeat in order to continue the adventure. Once all such guardians are defeated, the hero often enters a time of wandering, when very little seems to happen. For example, in the Hebrew Bible, Jonah sits in the belly of the whale pondering his future. A hero often experiences something that requires him to pause and deepen his understanding of his adventure. Soon, however, more interesting trials and adventures come, and often, supernatural friends show up to ease the passage. Finally, the quest is accomplished, the boon gained, and a hero finds him- or herself in a blissful period that is difficult to relinquish.

Eventually, though, the hero begins the return home, often with some rescue from without. Such supernatural aspects as a magic carpet often facilitate this return home, and guardians obstruct the return gateway, once more to be defeated. Successfully bringing home the gifts of the quest requires orchestrating the complexities of two worlds, integrating the gifts from the world of amplified power into day-to-day life. The hero then enters a time of waiting for the next call to adventure.

Young Alec, in the movie *The Black Stallion*, experiences the first stage of the hero's journey, the call to adventure, as he wanders aboard an ocean liner on a trip with his father. He is suddenly confronted with cloaked Arabic men beating a rearing, screaming stallion, whom they force into a dark enclosure. Later, drawn by the call to adventure that lies ahead of him, Alec sneaks back and sets sugar cubes for the horse on the ledge of a window in his stall.

In our own day-to-day lives, the call to adventure usually appears in a more mundane manner, and in fact we may not even recognize it as such until much later. It may come in the form of a phone call bearing news that shifts our lives forever. It may come as an accident or illness. It may come as a contest won or an honor bestowed. Whatever it is, we look back later and see it as the beginning of a journey into something new in our lives. Teens I have known in the residential treatment center look back and see that their calls to adventure were apprehension by the legal system for drug use, a confrontational argument with a parent, or other circumstances that landed them in the treatment center, offering them new tools and ways of being in the world.

A common reaction to the call to adventure is to say, No! All of us can recall a time when the call to adventure presented an unwelcome change, especially when heralded by something unpleasant such as an accident or illness. Sometimes it may show up simply as anxiety over a desired life change, such as the long-anticipated and hoped-for entry into one's chosen college, or the long-awaited sale of one's home. On arrival at our horse program, young people from the treatment center are sometimes still in the middle of that No! — resentfully going through their days and waiting until they can return to their previous lives or move on to something more of their own choosing. Although they remember having chosen the treatment center over jail time, they wrestle with affirming the call to adventure.

As we hear the call to adventure, allies often appear in our lives to help us along the way. For Alec, his father was a main ally. As allies do, Alec's father gave him two significant gifts that were important for him later. From his poker winnings, his father gave Alec a knife and a little horse statue with a story about how Alexander the Great tamed the wild stallion, Bucephalus, who carried him for years in his reign as king. In classical myths, the hero often sets forth with a magical sword, strange words of advice, or new friendships. In *The Lord of the Rings*, Frodo sets forth with Samwise Gamgee and two other Hobbits, to be joined later by Gandalf and Strider.

In our day-to-day lives, friends and loved ones gather to support us in new ventures, or we find ourselves meeting new acquaintances who are strangely suited to us at this time. It may be a significant doctor, a pet, or remarkable synchronicities that show up to support us in our new direction. William Hutchinson Murray, the Scottish mountaineer, remarked on this phenomenon:

> Until one is committed, there is hesitancy, the chance to draw back, always ineffectiveness. Concerning all acts of initiative (and creation), there is one elementary truth, the ignorance of which kills countless ideas and splendid plans: that the moment one definitely commits oneself, then Providence moves, too. A whole stream of events issues from the decision, raising in one's favor all manner of unforeseen incidents, meetings, and material assistance, which no man could have dreamt would have come his way. I learned a deep respect for one of Goethe's couplets: "Whatever you can do or dream you can, begin it. Boldness has genius, power, and magic in it!"[2]

At some point, the traveler on the hero's journey says yes to the path before him or her and crosses the threshold into a new realm of amplified experience. In classical stories demons and dragons often guard this threshold. Our hero must battle some challenge immediately. Frodo and his entourage evaded their first attack by the Dark Riders, who were drawn to the power of his ring. For Alec, a dramatic onboard fire forced him into the ocean with the black stallion as they crossed the threshold into their new life on a deserted island. In our own lives, this challenge often comes in the form of others questioning our new direction; parents and friends may insist that we are a bit crazy, or perhaps they fear for our safety. Or self-doubt may emerge, requiring us to clarify and strengthen our resolve to move ahead. Finally, though, we clearly step into the adventure that calls us, and like heroes before us, we step into this new experience feeling that we are indeed pioneering new territory for ourselves. However grudgingly or hesitantly, we step across a threshold into a new time. We begin a new project or turn in a new direction.

As mentioned above, once the hero has crossed this threshold, he or she often enters a time of quiet, when little or nothing seems to happen. This stage is classically referred to as the belly of the whale. Jonah is held in the belly of a whale as God gives him time to stop and prepare for the job before him. Alec awakens on a deserted island with the Black — bewildered, frightened, and in shock. He wanders about the island, grieving and quiet, retooling himself for the new landscape he has entered.

In our lives, when we start school or a new project, for instance, we may find ourselves caught in a seemingly interminable period, often years, of endless work requiring quiet but persistent discipline. Once we've launched ourselves into something new, we may find that the initial glamour wears off and we move ahead slowly indeed. This stage of the hero's journey often shows up as a time of depression and introspection, with little visible outward progress. This is not a clinical depression, although it may appear to be so. Instead it is a time of retooling the psyche on deep levels, preparing for the new times ahead.

Once our hero has done the work of inner retooling in the belly of the whale and gathered his allies on the journey, he or she embarks on a series of trials and adventures. Frodo and his companions battle orcs and narrowly escape the ghostly Dark Riders. Ulysses encounters a one-eyed giant and alluring Sirens. Alec discovers the black stallion caught in ropes and cuts him free with the knife provided by his father. As he wakes from a nap he encounters a cobra set to attack him. He discovers seaweed as a source of food for himself and the Black. He builds shelter for himself and finds ways to build a fire to cook fish he had caught laboriously. In our daily lives, we encounter unexpected challenges, regardless of how well we've planned things. On the student's journey, a teacher or professor may give impossible assignments. A new friend may enter our lives, bringing unexpected delights and diversions, or conversely, emotional upheaval that threatens to pull us off track. This part of the hero's journey is often full of stories told for the rest of one's life, handed down through generations, told and retold at family gatherings, and perhaps exaggerated for the benefit of those gathered around a campfire.

After many trials and adventures, our hero arrives at the place he or she sought. The knight finds the Holy Grail or defeats the dragon that has held his people hostage. The wanderer finds the treasure or a Shangri-la. It may be a holy marriage or some union with a divine being. It may be a spiritual initiation in which one experiences an expansiveness of being that was previously unknown. For our part, gaining the boon may be our time of finally finishing school or winning that first blue ribbon at a horse show. It may be a long-anticipated marriage or receipt of a wonderful gift. It may be a long-sought reconciliation with an estranged family member.

Vision quests are designed to allow us to embark on a hero's journey within a specific period, for the purpose of entering this place of discovery within ourselves to gain the boon that brings new and deeper purpose to our everyday lives. For Alec, his tireless efforts to make friends with the Black culminated in finally winning the Black's trust, so that he could climb onto the stallion's back and gallop down the beach, arms high in exuberance. That night, Alec and the Black lay together by a fire, the abused and wild stallion having befriended the boy who had taken the time to build a partnership instead of aggressively dominate him.

Eventually our hero must return home. The knight knows he must take back to his people the dragon's head, the treasure, or his new bride. Alec has made a livable situation for himself on the island by the time the crew on a fishing boat offers to take him home. Although eager to be rescued, he fights them off when he realizes they won't take the Black along too. For many heroes, it is often difficult to decide to return home when some outside force intervenes, sometimes in the form of a god, as in the case of Ulysses, other times with an outside circumstance, as with the fishermen who rescue Alec. For our part, for instance, we may find ourselves parked in neutral with the pleasure of being a perpetual student. We may find ways to perpetuate the honeymoon of romantic love, to stay in the warm womb of a friendship, to prolong the comfortable or the ecstatic. But a phone call comes announcing a new job opportunity, the last degree is earned, we have our first argument with our lover — something pulls us back to another part of our lives. And we return to a new version of our lives, bringing the realm of amplified power back to our everyday life. We find ways to bring the widened scope of our experience into the chores of daily living.

Alec finds himself returned to Chicago with the Black, but both of them are as fish out of water. He sits ill at ease in the school auditorium hearing corny poetry about his heroism. He eats at the dinner table with his hands and then goes to the backyard to share his salad with the Black, who is equally ill at ease in his new surroundings. The two of them sleep in the backyard. And yet Alec is delighted to be home with his mother again. He seeks ways to orchestrate the two worlds that he has known, city life and the island. He now encounters superficial human relationships, and is encumbered by words that come hard to him, in contrast to the nonverbal deep communication of movement and kinesthetic wisdom he knew with the Black in their island solitude. Similarly we find ways to build a marriage after the honeymoon phase is over. We weave the strands of patterns from earlier family life with threads from the deep bond forged in the fire of passionate love. Or having attained a hard-earned advanced degree, we now bring to our work new knowledge and vision to benefit the world.

In today's world we often find ourselves orchestrating a complex life with multiple worlds of family and friends, several jobs, hobbies, and sports. We may feel like we're wielding a giant TV remote, flipping through our life from one program to another. We're at the workplace; at home for parenting; at an event at our children's school; with another set of friends and acquaintances; out in the barn working with a horse and doing chores; and now and then fitting in a yoga class, book club, lecture, night class, or second job. Even when this phenomenon is not taken to such extremes, it is obvious that we live far more complex lives than previous generations. For example, after a day of travel with only a backpack full of clothes and equipment, a British reporter can attend a conference in San Francisco, type a story on his laptop computer at the local coffee shop, access the vast information stores of the Internet for relevant data with a few keystrokes, and then turn to email chats over a second cappuccino before instantly sending the revised report via email to the main office in London or Beirut. It is not uncommon now for a person to have two or more careers in a lifetime, with full honors accorded in each one. Medical schools and veterinary schools have an increasing number of older students, some in their forties and even fifties, who have decided to make a career change that would have been unheard of just forty years ago. The orchestration of our complex lives seems ever escalating. Along with the increased number of available opportunities, the fast-paced nature of our lives requires us to tap into deeper capacities that often lie dormant. We are called into new adventures to claim those capacities and embark on our own spiraling, circular hero's journey once more.

YOUNG PEOPLE from a residential treatment center attending my workshops on myth and the horse–human connection immediately understand that their time at the treatment center follows this mythic pattern. It is a revelation for them to see treatment as a hero's journey, full of unexplored promise and potential opportunities for the future. They are transformed when they view their entire lives, with the many ups and downs, as a powerful hero's journey. Instead of approaching their lives as problems to be solved, they rely on the hero's journey palette of tools to open pathways to hear and pursue the call of their highest selves, to listen to the yearning of their hearts and souls so they can realize their unfolding potential. When a student explores her particular adventure in partnership with horses, she gains new skills for sensitive communication, develops compassion as a potent tool for many life situations, and strengthens her capacity for trusting her intuition. Students begin to see horses as teachers, imparting skills to enhance their day-to-day lives. They find that they are indeed starring in a grand, exciting tale of their own. As a result, they begin to find ways to step more fully into the higher self that their adventures on horseback have allowed them to glimpse.

Unlike myths and stories patterned on the hero's journey, our own lives unfold in a less-than-linear manner, repeating a kind of ascending spiral pattern. We can discern the design in our overall life journey starting at birth and ending at death, and we can see it happening in our many short-lived adventures. As a mythic pattern, this design can apply to a single day's event, a challenging life period, a long-term process of personal growth, or one's entire life. It can offer much-needed perspective when we find ourselves slipping into desperate tunnel vision during a long period on the road of trials. It can help us understand how to benefit from the long, slow, and sometimes dark times in the belly of the whale. It can help us embrace the return home when it may be difficult to leave behind a period of ecstasy or profound discovery in the gaining of the boon.

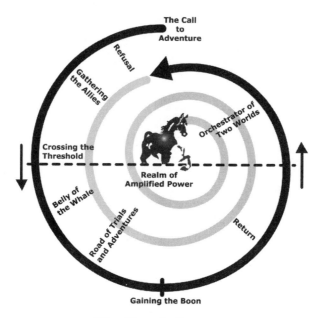

The Hero's Journey

ALTHOUGH THE MYTHIC FORM OF ANYONE'S LIFE tends to unfold with universal elements of the hero's journey, men and women
have historically taken different kinds of journeys, determined by numerous factors relating to gender differences in their personal and
societal roles. It is enlightening to explore how male and female brain
differences lend their unique pen strokes to the actual story line of
these journeys. It is only recently that scientists have been able to accurately view how men and women approach the same problem with
different parts of their brains firing, even when they come to the same
conclusions. Mona Lisa Schultz, MD, in her book *The New Feminine
Brain*, and Louann Brizendine, in *The Female Brain*, both outline
these differences and explore their implications for the future.

The primitive brains, the ones that we have had for tens of thousands of years, have served us well. They have allowed us to preserve
and expand our species and our world. Women were wired to find a
mate, create babies, and take care of others. Men were wired to
explore the outer world, to hunt, and to protect the women and

children from attack. The male response to danger was one of "fight or flight." But women with babies were unable to do that, so they developed "tend and befriend" as a response to danger. They have the fight-or-flight response too, but it is not as effective for women as it is for men. Thus, women developed other strategies for responding to danger, more indirect and based on talking and communicating.

These and other differences are laid down in a powerful enactment of a sort of hero's journey in the bodies of the mother and father long before birth. This does not ignore or discount other important factors surrounding us. We all have varying family and life circumstances that impinge on this story in significant ways. However, there is a basic scenario that we all participate in. Before conception, we're huddled as thousands of eggs in the mother's ovary, where we've been together for a long time, along with the brothers and sisters in the twin ovary on the other side of the mother's body. One or two eggs hear a call to adventure as they are chosen every month by a hormonal bath that sweeps through the mother's body. This chemistry matures a few of the eggs, so that some are stronger and ready, and get exploded out of the ovary and gathered by the filaments of the fallopian tube. At the same time the eggs travel down, the sperm are born fresh every twenty-four hours, with millions of buddies nested inside the testicles and nursed to maturity.

Then there is the great joining that brings the two together, the gaining of the boon. On their own hero's journey, the sperm barrel out of the gate with a pack of mitochondria on their backs like little backpacks of batteries, exploding into the cave of the womb. Some buddies get tired and stop as the others go on. At the same time, the gentle egg moves down the fallopian tubes, singing to the right sperm, calling to it. There are pictures of a whole group of sperm lining up to allow the right one to enter the egg, where it takes that solitary journey, inward past layers and layers of matter. Then begins another journey. The now-fertilized egg journeys into a vast open space, the cave that the sperm just navigated. It has seven days to find the right place in the wall of the cave, even as mitosis begins to enlarge the egg to more and more complexity. For the first eight weeks, the development of the brain is the same for both boys and girls. They are both bathed in estrogen, which builds connections throughout the brain. But then that Y chromosome in the boy emerges, creating a bath of testosterone that actually shrivels some of the connections begun with the estrogen so that boys do not have as many connections among parts of their brains.

At the end of three months, a slight shift in the chemistry occurs. The girl's communication centers and the corpus callosum, which is the bridging area between the right and left brains, grow stronger. The sexual and sensing centers grow bigger in boys. Because men need to have laser-like focus to be effective hunters, those skills at focusing are laid down early in the brain. The emotional and communication centers are not as large. Males are more easily able to shut down pain and shut off the connections with other people because, as hunters, they must be able to go away from home and be undistracted in their focus on the hunt.

Because the connection centers of the brain are different, connection to the mother is not the same with the boy as the girl. He is more separate. The girl remains in greater union with the mother because as females they share the same kind of nervous system, whereas the boy does not have that kind of nervous system. The boy prepares to explore the world, to play in it and learn his might and power. His success relies on his ability to compartmentalize things in his brain, to have fewer connections among brain areas, and to think about one thing at a time. He grows strong through venturing into his world and gaining recognition for his accomplishments there. The girl prepares to connect to the world and to other females. She has more connections among brain areas, compartmentalizes less, is better able to think about several things at a time, and has greater capacity for change. She needs to be mirrored by others' responses to her to know her true self, and needs to know that her presence affects others joyfully. This is true to a lesser extent with a boy, who will be an adventurer in the world, where his power accomplishes things. The girl is destined for a different kind of adventure, defined more by building relationships with others.

These inborn traits traditionally led men and women into different kinds of mythic journeys that had less to do with innate abilities than with different ways of perceiving the world. As Brizendine points out:

> We now know that when girls and boys first hit their teen years, the difference in their mathematical and scientific capacity is non-existent. . . . But as estrogen floods the female brain, females start to focus intensely on their emotions and on communication — talking on the phone and connecting with their girlfriends at the mall. At the same time, as testosterone takes over the male brain, boys grow less communicative and become obsessed about scoring — in games and in the backseat of a car. At the point when boys and girls begin deciding the trajectories of their careers, girls start to lose interest in pursuits that require more solitary work and fewer interactions with others, while boys can easily retreat alone to their rooms for hours of computer time.[3]

It is the perfect time for a young girl to bond with a horse and want to spend every moment at the barn. Riding is only one small part of the process in expressing the innate female talent for building connections. It can be just as satisfying to clean tack, shovel manure and spread shavings in the stall, or groom a horse who will immediately roll in the dirt at his first chance. These connections to a creature of large heart and mythic associations often take these young women into dreams and aspirations that, in later years, transfer to a wider scope of career and family. What begins as an adolescent expression of the hormonal trigger of feminine potencies for communication and connection often translates into work that calls for that same passionate bonding as a pediatrician, a psychotherapist, or an environmental activist.

Boys, too, follow their own mythic lure, but of a different sort. It is more often the physical action and challenge of competition that attracts them to horses, providing skills for later work in the competitive workplace. They are often not at all interested in talking about feelings or fostering communication. As the story goes, when the therapist conducting a couple's session asked the husband to say something about his feelings, he responded, "I feel like I want to watch the football game."

Another difference between men and women lies in their different ways of experiencing physical sensations. Women have more connections to the sensations within their own bodies and sometimes have a lower tolerance for pain. Men, on the other hand, are often wired with the ability to detach from pain, a skill necessary for the rigors of hunting and fighting. When women enter the male-dominated work world, they often require themselves to take on masculine traits such as ignoring messages from their bodies. They will ignore their innate feminine attention to their bodies' signals of pleasure or pain, to instead focus on the goals demanded for success in the workplace. In doing so, research shows, with this and other adaptations to the workplace, that women are actually changing their brain functioning. Men are making changes in their brains, too, when they assume the care of children and housekeeping while their wives earn high incomes in corporate positions. This exchange of roles challenges both men and women to develop their latent capacities and forge new evolutionary trends.

Everywhere today we can see individuals who have taken on the challenge of bridging these compelling hormonal differences. In *The Man Who Listens to Horses*, Monty Roberts tells a story of emerging from the historical, dominating male relationship with horses that his father had advocated, into a pioneering effort to accomplish the same results with horses in a far different manner after watching their herd behavior. Instead of "breaking" a horse in the traditionally brutal manner of his horse-trainer father, he found that he could accomplish better results with "join up," a method that relied on communicating with horses by using their own language. In doing so, he essentially rewired his own neural pathways by creating more circuits for connection and communication in the brain than his male forefathers had.[4]

Interestingly, we can see elements of this trend in our most urban communities. My friend, Denise Dignan, lives in Chicago and worked in the downtown area in the 1970s when the police were commonly referred to as "pigs"; this was during the civil rights era, when police beat up peaceful demonstrators at the Democratic convention. Downtown Chicago was not an area where most people wanted to be after dark; it was dangerous. Now, Denise tells me, Chicago is considered a renaissance city with a vibrant nightlife, where the police are seen throughout the area mounted on horses. They are no longer seen exclusively driving around in cars, where it was easy to polarize them as "pigs." When they ride horses through the city, they are more vulnerable, connected, and accessible to the people; and they have become part of a tide of change in Chicago in the past thirty years. The horses humanized the police in a way that the metal and speed of their cars could never have accomplished. Along with other measures instituted by the city, the mounted police support a fundamental shift to align the city and the police force with energy greater than the usual masculine approaches to law and order. The horses allow the people, both police officers and the citizens around them, to forge a new, more balanced approach to enforcing safety.

One of the negative consequences of the breakdown of traditional roles is that, by taking on masculine approaches, women can eclipse their more feminine traits, such as their connection with their bodies. They become more likely to suffer from depression, anxiety, other mood disorders, and a whole host of related physical ailments. Horses often bring them back to their bodies as they reach their thirties or forties. They may remember times on horseback as a child or recall unrealized dreams of such experiences. In any case, they find their way to a horse, through a friend's pasture, riding lessons, a workshop, or any number of circumstances. They find that horses restore them to who and what they really are, taking them on a hero's journey to claim the parts of themselves they had left behind.

Men, too, are finding that something new is being called for in the workplace to mediate the destructive effects of competition rooted somewhat in their masculine heritage. They seek new approaches to situations of conflict and stress common in the corporate world that lead to early heart attacks, stroke, and other breakdowns in health, not only for employees but organizations as well. The Institute of HeartMath has taken a scientific approach to developing and testing more heart-centered activities for these environments. More common in Europe than in the United States, former corporate executives who have turned to corporate consulting increasingly work with horses as an especially effective way to communicate more heart-based strategies for the workplace.

Years ago I recognized that people came to horses seeking something more than success in the show arena. I began to seek ways of providing motivating experiences for riders without creating competitive situations with winners and losers. I believe in competition because it encourages and energizes striving for our personal best. But so much of what occurs in our schools, our sports, and our society creates situations in which one person's personal best is configured at the expense of someone else, the loser. Or the competitive goal takes precedence over the well-being of the competitor and the well-being of our equine partners, as witnessed in the number of race horses run prematurely at two years of age, causing them to face a lifetime of damaged joints and psyches.

As a child and adolescent, and even in college, I eagerly participated in competitive sports and classroom situations. I was fortunate that such situations allowed me more winning than losing, so my self-esteem remained fairly intact. However, as an undergraduate in premedical classes at a large university, I began to question the premises of this system. It seemed fairly obvious to me that to follow this competitive spirit to its logical conclusion resulted in war and other destructive eventualities, in which the losers were whole populations instead of a few classroom students at the bottom of the bell-curve chart. There are countless ways that our society unwittingly emphasizes rating ourselves in comparison to others instead of using more beneficial parameters such as creatively applying that knowledge to achieve new solutions to old problems, among other more-valuable goals.

Yet it is hard to imagine a world in which some kind of competition would not figure prominently. We thrive on certain aspects of competition, such as exploring and seeking to attain our dreams and goals for a better world or life for ourselves and our families. I suspect that it is inherent in what it means to be human. I grew up in the flat, red lands of Oklahoma, where I frequently found my thoughts unwinding into the horizons that lay far, far in the distance. That landscape evoked a yearning to explore the unknown just beyond that far horizon, and provided an outward landscape for my inner unfolding. Just as horses were the beginning of my spiritual connection with beauty, movement, and the natural world, the long, flat landscapes of Oklahoma beckoned me to venture forth into a larger world. Fundamental patterns were emerging for my future years. The books I chose to read supported that searching spirit, as did my hours on horseback, riding the trails that led out from the stable. I competed in school to get ahead and get out into that world.

When I began to travel into the larger world, over and over I found that life does not have to be configured in terms of win or lose. It is so often a win-win situation, viewed through eyes seeking that outcome. I sought ways to teach this to my students.

The initial phase of learning the basics of riding provides students with plenty of challenge. But with the long routine of practice, entropy can set in, potentially bringing boredom. A typical solution is to enter into competition to wake up everyone and give some charge to the repetitive work necessary for strong riding skills. This encourages the mind-set, "You've got to do this hard work so you'll win at a horse show."

I knew there had to be a better way. I developed adventure games as a tool for me and other instructors to work specifically at a mythic and symbolic level and, by doing so, consciously activate all the other levels of the self. The games give riders the opportunity to develop their imaginations and to step into the mythic world for a short time, playing out brief heroes' journeys. The games begin to lay the foundation for students to take the stage of their own lives. In this way, these games are not an escapist fantasy or an effort to avoid the realities of life. Instead their intent is to lead one back into life with more passion and courage. A myth speaks to one's body and higher self, engendering wisdom about the way life really is, while a fantasy tends to give voice to imagined fears and strategies to overcome them.

There is one important precaution: since many students tend to want to "kill the enemy" and become competitive and aggressive, we carefully design the games so that when they encounter obstacles along the way, game rules require that they must find other ways to approach the "enemy." Whether it is Darth Vader, a dragon, Batman's or Superman's foes, or anything fearful, they generally must ask what the enemy needs, then respond to what they hear by finding ways to work out a cooperative solution so that the rider can move on. We choose stories that do not emphasize good guy–bad guy dimensions, but instead work with the idea that we are all on a hero's journey of mythic proportions with obstacles offering life lessons and gifts along the way. Classical and modern myths often embody this dynamic of the human journey, and are a rich resource for stories.

Buddhist practices call this approach to the enemy "feeding your demons." It is a practice that recognizes that engaging in battle with demons, either inner or outer, often perpetuates a dualistic approach to matters that can be better approached in another way. Tsultrim Allione, Buddhist author of *Women of Wisdom* and founder of the retreat center Tara Mandala, has based her training program, Feeding Your Demons, on the work of eleventh-century woman yogini Machig Lapdron. Instead of plunging heroically into the fight against our inner or outer problems, she encourages us to explore another choice. We can talk with our interior demons. We can recall incidents of the recent past when we experienced anger, sorrow, jealousy, exhaustion, uncertainty, anxiety, or stoicism — any kind of upset. We look at where that pain is located in our body and notice how it feels. Then we try to visualize what it looks like. What does the demon of anxiety, jealousy, or fear look like? The next step is to ask the demon from the heart, in a spirit of love, "What do you need?" It may be helpful for just a moment to vividly imagine ourselves as the demon, to more directly feel what the demon needs so that we can better hear the answer. Once we listen carefully to what the demon says, then we imagine ourselves possessing plenty of what is needed. We feed the demon lavishly, with an abundant spirit. We give it all the love, attention, tenderness, and understanding that it needs. The demon indulges itself and takes the offering hungrily. We feed it without reservation until it is completely content and fulfilled. Then we observe how the demon has changed, how its neediness is diminished.[5]

Jamie Sams and David Carson's book *Animal Medicine* treats the same subject with a charming story from Native American traditions: Deer represents the ability to transform anything blocking our way to our sacred goal. In this case a fawn has heard a call from Great Spirit to go to the top of Sacred Mountain. There, the fawn encounters a horrible demon who tries to keep all beings from connecting with Great Spirit. This very frightening demon combines all the ugly monsters that have ever been. But the fawn responds to the demon in the spirit of gentleness, with compassion and love, and simply requests,

"Please let me pass. I'm on my way to see Great Spirit." Similar to the blustery Wizard of Oz, no matter how hard he tries to muster ugliness, to his dismay the demon finds that his hardened, ugly heart has been penetrated and so he melts. He shrinks to the size of a walnut, and from then ever after, all beings are able to make the connection to Great Spirit. "Deer teaches us to use the power of gentleness to touch the hearts and minds of wounded beings who are trying to keep us from Sacred Mountain. Like the dappling of Fawn's coat, both the light and the dark may be loved to create gentleness and safety for those who are seeking peace."[6]

Conflict is a given in any good story and in anyone's life. Conflict raises the stakes in any situation, calls forth our energy, and triggers all kinds of adrenaline and pheromones that can feel exciting. The intent of the adventure games is to harness that energy and focus it on productive instead of destructive solutions. In real life, when we resist killing our enemy and instead seek to attend to his or her needs while honoring our own, we contribute to an evolutionary step desperately needed at all levels of our human community. It is hard work, but the repercussions of not doing so are dire, and with some practice, it becomes an artful and delightful approach to tough issues.

TRY THIS

Preparing for the Larger Journey with Adventure Games

Adventure games are popular with riders of all ages and ability levels, and are an effective way to begin exploring the power of myth and to prepare for understanding the hero's journey aspect of one's life. Essentially the adventure game is a miniature hero's journey. A few examples are shared here to seed the possibilities for many more. I have found that students soon arrive with their own stories they want to act out, such as favorite movies, action games, or even Bible stories. Also, stories can be designed to address particular issues in students' lives or current situations happening in their communities. When you tease the mythic elements of the hero's journey out of these stories, then you can find ways to set up an adventure game that allows others to experience personally the power of the story for their own lives. Although the first two games are configured for a group situation from my teaching experience, the third offers you the opportunity to create your own version, as it may apply to a current situation in your life. The game becomes a symbolic drama for rehearsing a new story for you. Acting out a story that offers new alternatives to your usual way of doing things, or even acting out an alternative, preferred version of a past experience, can be a surprisingly simple and effective way to harness the power of myth for your own life. It also offers a way for you to practice incorporating a more enlightened approach to conflict into your own life — to practice feeding the demons, as discussed earlier in this chapter.

GOALS

- Maintain or accelerate your attention, interest, and focus.
- Integrate and deepen previously learned riding skills.
- Empower yourself to approach life challenges in a new, more effective way.
- Enact playfully your own possible mythic life stories.

SCENARIO 1: HEROIC TALES

Adventure games are often best played at the end of any riding lesson in which specific riding skills were practiced using the poles, cones, and other items in the arena.

PREPARATION AND EQUIPMENT

You will need the following items to create a simple obstacle course:

- Large orange cones in a line, six strides apart (to represent a mountain range)
- A set of colored cones lined up eight strides apart (to represent a rainbow forest)

- A maze constructed of jump poles or ten to twenty lengths of fourteen-foot PVC pipe with several turns in and out (for a cave or labyrinth)
- Parallel poles or cavalettis placed four feet apart (for a river to be crossed)
- A basketball net mounted on a pipe frame (for a mountaintop)

The instructor selects or makes up a story and creates a role for the rider to play in it. For instance, in a variation on Jack and the Beanstalk, there may be several foam blocks covered with gold velour ("stolen bricks of gold") stuffed into the basketball net (the mountain or volcano), and the rider's mission is to return them home.

Be sure to familiarize the horses with all items, as well as activities, that might be included in these games.

Time: Highly variable, fifteen to forty-five minutes

The instructor steps into a playful role in the story, such as that of a queen whose gold has been stolen or lost. She knows it has been hidden at the top of the mountain in the distance (pointing to the basketball net) and asks Sir Andrew (or other made-up name for the rider) to bring it back. He must ride through a particular "landscape" to get there and back; for instance, through the forest, over the river (with imaginative enhancements; for example, if the horse's feet hit the poles, that means he fell in the water), through the mountain range and the maze, finally to arrive at the mountain, where he will find the gold. Review the rules for encountering obstacles; that is, ask what the enemy wants and then provide it.

The rider is sent out on his or her mission with surprises or obstacles along the way, as suitable for each rider's issues. For example, a shy rider who seldom talks will often eagerly tell a dragon (usually an instructor in disguise) that he wants to get by, and then ask the dragon what he needs. The dragon may say that he needs a drink of water for his fiery breath, and soon the rider has found him a drink (with the help of some handy volunteers) and goes on his way with a huge grin on his face. Older, more sophisticated riders might be challenged by an impossible demand, so that they can be coached in how to negotiate a compromise. In therapeutic riding programs, there are usually a number of volunteers who gladly take various roles and often lend their own suggestions. However, it is important that volunteers also be briefed in how to approach obstacles so that they do not unwittingly lapse into the usual superhero scenario of killing the enemy.

Volunteers can be asked to lead new riders and riders with disabilities. Side walkers, who support their riders in a therapeutic riding situation, can be given a role such as Samwise Gamgee from *The Lord of the Rings*, whose job is to help the rider along the way. Or they may become the wings of Pegasus, helping the riders to fly into their quest.

This game adapts well to a group lesson in which students are sent on their own individual quests, tailored for their own riding-skill levels so that they can negotiate the mountains and rivers with others in a timely fashion. The elements of the hero's journey provide structure and meaning to the activities. It may be helpful to imagine that the game is a call to adventure from the instructor to the rider, so that it is explained with appropriate emphasis on the rider's heroic role. The rider decides who the accompanying allies will be on this adventure and gives new names and roles to the assisting volunteers. It may help to create a crossing of the threshold with a verbal announcement or by placing two parallel poles on the ground to form a gateway into the rest of the ride. Great celebration can accompany attainment of the goal, or the gaining of the boon. And finally, bringing the boon back home is greeted with gratitude and affirmation of its importance.

SCENARIO 2: CITIZENS IN THE LOCAL COMMUNITY

You can use adventure games to encourage and teach good citizenship. In these games, young riders are given roles that deal with a current community issue and pattern their future roles as responsible and capable citizens in their communities, evoking positive approaches to problematic situations.

For example, forest fires are a persistent concern in our community in the Pacific Northwest. During one season when fires clouded the skies and stories circulated about threats to wildlife, we created the following adventure game.

PREPARATION AND EQUIPMENT

- Distribute fifteen to twenty stuffed animals around the riding arena so that they can be reached from horseback, for example, on ledges or tied to poles. It's best to have a great deal of variety in colors and types of animals.
- Use a large hula hoop, jump poles, or PVC pipes to designate one or more small areas at one end of the arena.
- If desired, you can arrange the poles and cones in the arena for landscape features, as in Scenario 1, "Heroic Tales," above.

The instructor or leader announces that the forest fires have caused many animals in the forest to flee and that they are scattered and lost in areas that have no food and water for them. They need some help: to be brought to a place where food and water are plentiful, or to be relocated to another forested area where they can thrive. Riders can be enlisted to help decide what needs to be done to remedy the situation. They are deputized as forest rangers and sent out with various assignments, perhaps to gather all the brown, black, or white animals; or all the cats, dogs, cows, or horses. A rider's job may be to bring the animals back to the designated areas where they will have food and water. These areas are defined by hula hoops or poles. Various challenges can be introduced with the objects in the arena so that riders must practice the riding skills they are currently working on.

When I started adventure games with my students with disabilities, I realized that we had stepped into something new and important.

Students taking other lessons at the opposite end of the arena would stop and watch. The excitement was palpable. Able-bodied students' instructors approached and asked if their students could join the fun. They had never seen anything like it. Instructors asked me to give in-service trainings so that they could incorporate these games into their own lessons. I found that even the most profoundly autistic students insisted on including an adventure game as part of their lessons. It was clear that students integrated riding skills as they developed on psychological and spiritual levels. Riders returned to their everyday lives with renewed inspiration, having touched some vital aspect of themselves during their experience with the horses. We had entered into the power of myth, and they had experienced a taste of their own hero's journey.

SCENARIO 3: RIDING INTO A NEW FUTURE

A simple way to experience this power for yourself is to make a trail ride into an adventure game. You can take with you the elements of a troubling situation in your life, and find symbolic representations along the way out. You can give a person standing in your way the role of a large boulder at the side of the trail. You can attribute a sense of confusion to a cluster of trees that you have to navigate through on your horse, allowing your meandering to evoke that feeling of confusion. At some point, usually on the return trip, you allow the landscape to reveal some new understanding about the situation. You and your horse might encircle the grove of trees, while you watch for new and clarifying perceptions in this new approach. You might avoid the boulder in the trail by taking an entirely different route, as you explore how you might find similar ways to deal with a difficult person. Your horse's response to things along the way can offer illuminating challenges for working with associates. You can perhaps see how your current situation reflects one stage of your own hero's journey. Aside from the power of engaging a current situation in a symbolic form that can yield new insight, another major reason for the power of this activity lies in engaging your body in the story, physically pursuing your search for a fresh perspective or new solution. When you bodily engage yourself in your own story in this imaginative way, especially with a horse, you begin to enter into the power of myth for your own life.

IN THE FOLLOWING CHAPTERS we will explore various aspects of the hero's journey as they are demonstrated in story and in day-to-day life. Changing the names of real-life characters, we will explore various issues involved in living your mythic life and stories to enrich your experience as you open to this aspect of your life. If you have horses in your life, you will have the opportunity to develop various skills in powerful activities that will enhance your ability to enter your mythic life more fully. Happy trails!

CHAPTER THREE

HORSES FOR PARTNERSHIP AND NEW ADVENTURE

Attuning Yourself to Subtle Communication

PART OF WHAT IT MEANS TO BE HUMAN is to yearn for partnership. We emerge from the most intimate of all partnerships when we are born from our mother's womb, that most primal call to adventure. We find ourselves encapsulated in flesh and blood, with intimations of immortality whispering in our ears from a place outside time, where we once knew a connection with something more. We spend much of our time pursuing that connection, whether in our relationships with other people or in our search for something more in everyday life. This search makes for extraordinarily good stories.

Horses stepped into people's lives centuries ago, straight out of the realm of partnership, lending their physical power and assistance to us in all kinds of endeavors. Their subtle style of expressing themselves elicited a new palette of communication skills from those human partners seeking more than a domineering relationship. The

Arabian peoples of *The Black Stallion* bred their horses for the ability to literally live in the tents with their nomadic families, as well as for their superior skills in providing transportation for daily life and battle in a desert landscape. As a result, Arabian horses developed into compact, intelligent, expressive, and unusually interactive partners in their human communities. Long passages of the Koran are dedicated to their beauty and universal, supernatural power. "I have given thee the power of flight without wings!" sings God about his gift of the horse to man.

Today, when we have the opportunity to be introduced to horses, we enter into an adventure of a new, unique partnership in which that intimate connection so honored in the desert world takes on a new and important role in our lives. Our connection with horses becomes a seminar in subtle communication. In contrast to historical relationships with horses, which were often based on dominating the horse — for battle, farmwork, transportation, sport, competition — you will now find books, videos, and clinics offering a glimpse into a new partnership, in which we must awaken parts of ourselves that can respond to the demands before us. This begins with awakening our senses for more acute attunement with the world around us and learning to listen to subtle cues in our bodies. Horse whisperers have become famous for their skill in this partnership. Though we have observed tragic instances to the contrary from unskillful practices, it is a partnership that our entire planet is growing into. Our very existence relies on finding ways to cross cultural barriers of all kinds and enter into partnerships for greening the earth. When we learn how to cross the barriers between species by communicating with a horse, we contribute to that riverbed of our ancestors that carries us into the future of a global community where we dwell in the awareness and honoring of all life forms. Horses become our Gaian teachers and partners.

As a child I was fortunate to have known Ara Smith. His business card read, "Why let any old horse trader cheat you on a horse?

Let me do it." His dry sense of humor and gentle but effective way with horses was a magnet to young people, like me, with horses in their blood. Ara and his wife, Rose, became our second parents, now and then teaching us in preparation for local horse shows and hauling our horses to local show facilities each summer. But even when they were not actively teaching, we learned from them. Medium built, with a preference for overalls to the usual Levis, Ara handled his two stallions in a calm but firm manner, which was particularly challenging with the two-year-old stud colt, Duke, who was in training to replace King, the older breeding stallion. Ara knew how to assert his leadership with these and other horses in a way that invited their trust and participation in human activity. He met Duke's simmering, testosterone-charged behavior with a quiet but firm insistence, inviting the colt to participate in the world around him rather than head for an explosive outburst.

In contrast, I later witnessed more than a few show trainers who took an approach that forced submission of their horses through brute force. The horses were made to conform to the human standards of show ring performance, instead of being offered a future that would best suit their talents and inclinations.

Interacting with horses gives us a rare opportunity to mindfully cultivate true partnership. Increasingly today, as we respond to the needs of our world and become more conscious, the same horses that were previously forced into submission are now honored as sentient beings that provide a whole host of possible interactions. This new kind of partnership with the horse presents us with many challenges. For one thing, we must take into account the fact that horses are animals and that historically we have taken them out of their natural environment, where they ran freely in herds over large prairies. We have enlisted them in human endeavor. Recognizing that fact means that our partnership with them began with our choice rather than theirs. However, unlike other wild animals, horses, like dogs and cats, have chosen to agree to and enter into the partnership. This means that we have considerable responsibility to honor their choice with gratitude and respect. However, it does not mean that, out of that gratitude, or even guilt, we allow ourselves to become ineffective leaders or passive in the face of aggressive behavior by the horse, allowing the horse to take charge of a situation and possibly harm himself or people. Nor does that attitude of gratitude and respect imply that we should overlook the unique equine nature that distinguishes the horse from people and other animals.

People who are new to horses sometimes wish to act in a more enlightened manner with them, and thereby expect horses to think and behave like humans. They become frustrated when the horse does not respond to requests that people, or even a pet such as a dog, understand. This is anthropomorphism, and it looks something like this: A horse's owner hangs a holiday stocking full of apples on her horse's stall door, but within reach of the horse next door, who could extend his head through the open area of the stall door. Within minutes the wrong horse finds the treat and munches his way through all the apples. The owner is furious that the neighboring horse did not respect her admonishment to leave the apples alone. She insists that horses can be expected to respect the wishes of people.

Here is another example of misguided expectations of the horse: Like most horse owners, this lady expects her horse to lead through the outdoors without constantly pulling for grass at the side of the road. This works fine until a day when she is especially pleased with her horse's performance in the ring. After the ride, she takes him outside to let him graze as a reward for his good work. The next day, she's angry with him when he pulls on the lead rope to enjoy a few bites of grass as he had the day before. She thinks he should understand that grass eating is only a reward for good arena performance. With these and similar scenarios, she leads her horse into confusion and misbehavior rather than partnership.

Probably one of the most common situations a trainer faces is a new adult rider who purchased a first horse about six months previously, a solid-citizen sort of horse, gentle and well trained, who has turned into a spoiled brat, or worse, a dangerous bully. The new owner admits to feeding treats and offering lots of love and affection. She reports noticing that the horse very gradually has become more and more disobedient. Before long, out on the trail the horse decides he'd rather head back to the barn, so he tosses his head high, grabs the bit in his teeth, and takes off. Or he surges ahead when led, and responds to correction with lots of head tossing, dancing around, and generally making a ruckus over what should be routine matters.

In some ways, I like natural-horsemanship trainer Julie Goodnight's sassy approach to these matters:

> It is your job, as leader of the herd, to provide for food, water, and shelter; keep discipline in the herd; and to alert the herd to danger. What your horse gives you in return for all of this is not his love, but his unconditional indifference. Get used to it; he's not a dog. But if you are worthy of being his leader, he will also look up to you, be obedient and respectful toward you, and want to be with you all the time and go anywhere with you for the comfort and security that you provide. It reminds me of one of my favorite jokes. Definitions, as written by the horse: Owner — human assigned to feed me. Trainer — owner with mafia connections. Farrier (horseshoer) — human on which I can take out all of my pent-up frustration without compromising my food source.[1]

What I am suggesting, however, is that this leadership does not stop at training a horse to be obedient and respectful and to want to be with the owner for comfort and security. Leading the horse to partnership takes the relationship a step farther for other mutually beneficial purposes.

Obviously this does not condone forcing a horse into work that he clearly and consistently refuses, or that he obediently undertakes with little interest, which is a common situation with competitive show horses, who may have the good looks and athleticism for a sport but not the temperament. There is a delicate line between aggression and assertiveness. One of the earliest lessons new riders, especially girls and women, often must learn is how to be appropriately and calmly assertive with a horse, to exert the authority to call him back into partnership. To be safe and successful with horses, new riders must learn the difference between appropriate assertiveness and abusive aggression. Females are often well taught in our culture to avoid being aggressive, and in the process, they have not learned the benefits of appropriate assertiveness. With a horse, however, to have the benefits of long-term safe and rewarding riding, those habits must eventually be addressed. Riders must learn a variety of skills necessary for leading the horse to partnership. Along with learning the riding skills taught by a skilled instructor, they can enhance those skills by learning to work with subtle energies and body language to gain an understanding of the horse's instinctual responses. These lessons in partnership bring new energy to performance in the ring or on the trail. Also, they translate for the rider into greater ease and wisdom when conflict arises in human social situations, so that they can use intuition and compassion in practical situations, opening undeveloped human capacities.

This relationship may seem rather obvious, but if you spend time at training facilities for competition in jumping, racing, cutting-horse events, endurance riding, or any number of other competitive events, you will find that the practice of responding to horses in this manner is often compromised. Providing a winner to a high-paying customer at least occasionally takes precedence over other standards. Partnership pales to insignificance because in these situations trainers often simply look for how well the horse obeys the person working with him. Missing from the situation is how to honor the horse's sentient nature, and how to have the horse and rider work together in a synergistic manner, with give and take on both sides. This approach concerns how a goal set by a human being, such as maneuvering through an obstacle course, is treated as a point for conversation between horse and human, rather than the one and only acceptable outcome for the interaction. Partnership requires that skills be laid down for listening and responding on both sides of the interaction, crossing the lines that often separate us from other species, which teaches us how to build bridges among people, and even cultures, in the process.

One horse, named Dollar, taught me a good bit about walking the fine line between assertive partnership and aggression. I had been looking for another lesson pony for my able-bodied students in San Antonio when I came across him. I was attracted to him because he looked like a very well-built show horse rather than a pony, measuring a mere 13.2 hands, and he was, as the horse trader had said, "sound as a dollar." His perky disposition attracted me too.

However, his previous owner, a ten-year-old girl, had been afraid of him. Dollar would not do a flat walk, but instead would jig with nervous energy, and would repeatedly dump riders by refusing to jump at the last minute. A bit wild-eyed about being ridden, though he did not buck or rear, he seemed to burst with anxiety that prevented him from walking. He very likely gave his young owner the sense that he was about to run away at any moment. This particularly escalated whenever he came near a jump in the arena. He also swerved into the middle of the ring at a trot and stopped suddenly, unseating a young rider. And worse, he ran sideways when not in the arena, taking even an adult rider and himself back to the barn and his stall.

Clearly Dollar would not fit into my teaching program unless I could enlist his cooperation to work together with me and my students. According to reports, his previous trainer had punished him for these behaviors. This obviously had not accomplished the desired goal, and instead had raised the level of his anxiety to the point where he finally had been turned over to a horse trader. I ended up buying him for a pittance.

I began asserting our desire for a partnership with him by meeting his misbehavior with nonabusive resistance. For instance, my assistants and I made sure that when a rider was mounted on Dollar on the way to the arena, a strong leader led him to prevent his dashes back to the barn. After a few weeks of this, Dollar walked in a relaxed manner with a leader, and after several months, we cautiously allowed our more experienced riders to ride him unaccompanied to the arena, with total and continued success from then forward. At the same time, weeks of riding him daily, and patiently and consistently asking quietly for only a flat walk finally resulted in a relaxed but energetic, sensitive, and willing pony, one who could trust that he was not going to elicit angry punishment for anxious behavior. More challenging to address were his unexpected swerves into the middle of the ring, breaking away from a trotting group of riders. Typical of his intelligence, knowing that he could not succeed, he never tried the tactic with a larger rider.

This was about the time we decided to change Dollar's name to Foxfire, a more descriptive name for his personality — classy, foxy, and fiery. We realized that if riders were going to partner with this little guy, they would have to meet him on his own ground, so to speak. Passively riding him at a trot and hoping he would follow his herd instinct, or shrieking in panic when he began to swerve, did not result in a happy rider. These young riders began to learn their first lessons in asserting themselves through their bodies — hands, legs, and weight — along with their voices, the moment Foxfire gave them the slightest hint that he was about to swerve. They met his desire to swerve with their own desires to stay in the groups. You could see the conversation go on, with Foxfire deciding, "Well, okay," as he would settle back into the group. Within a few months, Foxfire became our most popular mount. His anxious misbehavior matured into a nimble eagerness we could rely upon in the enclosed riding arena, and a bold happiness when leading a group out on the trail. After a few years, he even returned to carrying young riders over jumps with equanimity.

Learning this kind of partnership best begins on the ground, off the horse's back. We can enter a pasture or stall with our horse and begin a give-and-take dance, of sorts, in which leadership lies between the two, human and horse. The language of the mind gives way to a language that lies in the heart and the body. We can develop the tools to maintain that cooperative partnership so that no one is harmed and, in fact, there is a sense that we are participating in beneficial activities for all concerned, horses and humans.

Horses can sometimes underscore this in quite amazing ways so that we come to realize that we often are led into partnership at least as much as we lead. One morning we had just finished a game in our large arena with a group of eight teenage girls and two trusted horses, a mare and a gelding, who were loose in the arena. The game had required the girls to find ways to partner with the horses without touching them or bribing them with food, so that the horses would cross over a small barrier. It took forty-five minutes to accomplish this. They learned that coercion would not work when the horses had a choice of just walking away or simply standing still. They had to enlist the horses' cooperation. They had to create partnerships. Fourteen of us, students and staff, gathered in a circle in the middle of the arena to reflect on the girls' experiences and discuss how they had finally met the challenge. The horses were still loose in the arena, one at each end of the space, a good distance away from us.

Immediately as we gathered, the mare, Madison, who had been the most difficult for the girls to enlist in their game, strolled over to the group and walked into our circle, placing herself shoulder to shoulder with the rest of us. Amused at her behavior, we acknowledged her presence and welcomed her to listen to our discussion, speculating tongue in cheek that she might perhaps have something to contribute. We talked for about fifteen minutes, and Madison stood quietly the whole time. In conclusion, I began to tell the young women about the heritage of Arabian horses and that they had been bred to live amicably in the tents with the families who owned them, a tent possibly about the size of the space we had created with our circle. Just as I said these words, Madison moved for the first time in over fifteen minutes. She took a few steps forward and placed herself squarely in the center of our circle, as if to say in response to my words, "Just like this!" There was not a single person present that day who did not go away in delight and wonder at Madison's participation, which confirmed beyond our usual reckonings the beneficial possibilities of partnership with horses.

FOR SOME OF US, HORSES CALL US TO ADVENTURE. The call often comes in our early years, only to be responded to years later, perhaps even as an adult, with other adventures intervening along the way. It may come in that first sight of the grace and movement of a horse galloping across a field. Or it may come in that first, sensational experience of simply walking atop the back of a pony or horse, which gives our body's habitual movements something new and larger, the promise of new horizons opening for us. Whenever the seed of the horse's call to adventure is sown, we have many opportunities to respond to that call as our lives unfold.

Years ago, I experienced a call to adventure that changed my professional career. At that time I had taught riding and trained horses for eight years in San Antonio, with the largest youth riding program in the city. By then, I had spent several years developing my own style of teaching young people and adults to enjoy trail riding and successfully compete in local horse shows. In the summertime I conducted a day camp for beginning riders and a more advanced format for experienced riders.

On the other hand, during that time I had become increasingly uncomfortable with the horse-show world. Although I coached my students to pursue competition to attain their personal best, I was aware that there were many questionable premises in the structure of the shows that we participated in. My riders often entered a show ring with a group of eight to fifteen riders, all jostling for the judge's attention or hiding from the judge when their horse misbehaved. Because of this structure, winning horse-and-rider teams often committed errors while the judge's back was turned. Riders were lured into competing against one another in the ring instead of riding against an objective standard of excellence, which, in my mind, was the proper focus in their training. In addition, the horses supported by a rider's wealthy parents' funds were sure to win over even the hardest-working rider without such funds. Money ruled over hard work and skill.

One day I headed for a riding lesson with a group of students and found myself thinking about how I truly wanted my life to make a positive difference in the world. Even though horses were a lifesaving presence in the lives of some of my students, the availability of horses was limited to the affluent. Those who could really benefit from horses — those in poverty, the inner city, or broken homes — were not able to experience them.

I admired people who had a special expertise and made something significant of it, such as the extreme example of a severely burned Vietnam veteran I'd met, who inspired thousands of schoolchildren with his stories of coming back from his horrific injuries. With severe burns that covered all of his face and left him with prosthetic hands and feet, David Jayne had gone on to law school and a successful practice in corporate law. That day, as I recalled his inspiration, I suddenly realized that one thing I did have in my bones was my understanding of horses and riding. Right then, I decided to find a way to develop that expertise in a direction that would make a difference. Looking back on that ordinary day, I know nobody noticed that I had just made a life-changing decision, that I had heard a call to adventure. I hardly noticed it myself, but I did notice that it felt so right. It was a thought that I could grow with. And so I did. After that, I was attentive to possible avenues for accomplishing a new direction for my work that would make a positive difference.

During this time I developed an adventure camp for my advanced riders. We explored a different culture every two days, learning on horseback about each culture's unique gifts to the human journey. In one scenario, we sat under a tree, eating pickled cactus, and heard mythic stories of the medicine wheel of Native American lore, tying them into the very landscape on which we sat. Then each person chose an animal totem for the week, explored the meaning of that totem for a current life situation, and painted it onto a cloth that would later serve as a bareback pad. During the Native American sessions, riding took place in our huge indoor arena, and riders mounted their horses with only a neck rope — no saddle or bridle. These students were advanced enough and their horses well trained enough that this activity took them all to an exciting edge of challenge. With a simple obstacle course, a miniature version of what it meant to ride the plains and mountains of the American West, students tasted on horseback the intimate, spiritual connection with the natural world that is one of the gifts of that culture. Without the usual aids of bridle and saddle, they also, of course, learned to communicate more effectively with their horses using their whole bodies.

At Adventure Camp, we explored China and the Eastern world, the ancient Celtic world, India, and ancient Greece, among others. Although the history of the horse's role with mankind tied these experiences together, we consciously gleaned the gifts of the past to benefit a new future emerging for horses and humans in today's world. The horse is no longer man's necessary tool for work or transport. The new role emerging from their more recent use for recreation and sport honors horses as participating partners, sentient beings with unique gifts for higher purposes. The horse calls us to a new adventure. More than compliant partners for a human agenda, horses have begun to gain recognition for the large heart and sensitivity that are part of their birthright. They are taking on their own role as teachers of sensitive communication and leadership that honors partnership with all concerned, giving us a new perspective on our world, our own lives, and the potential for working in cooperative partnerships for world-changing situations. This results in better-skilled riders who can appreciate the horse for teaching them how to deal with difficult situations in their daily lives, for bringing more of themselves to interactions and situations, and for moving successfully into the skills of an adept full being — body, mind, and spirit.

IN ANSWERING ANY CALL TO ADVENTURE with a horse, everyone, including the horse, must be safe. That safety involves how to conduct oneself around a horse in basic activities on the ground before mounting. These basic skills of horse handling must not be neglected when one aspires to engage a horse in other, subtler endeavors. Because we are building a partnership with a horse, the basic activities of haltering, leading, grooming, and riding are also a training ground for the fundamental skills for practicing compassion, working confidently with our intuitions, and practicing discernment in complex interactions with others whom we may not understand well. When we enter into this kind of partnership with a horse, it is important to learn how to use our usual horsemanship skills in a manner that safely builds and ensures that partnership.

First we can observe and try to understand the horse's style of expression and way of understanding the world. When a horse has not shut down to cope with his world, he is extremely sensitive to his environment. Watch a horse at play with others, and you will notice the radar-like antenna of the horse's ears moving about as he tunes in to all around him. You will notice the quality of his eyes as they open widely in fear or startlement, or close halfway as he relaxes. His body language demonstrates his instinctual tendency for flight, freeze, or fight. For a dog, the tail is its main mood indicator. The horse's tail gives signals too, with a different meaning: it will be clamped tightly between his legs in irritation or discomfort, rapidly swung up and down in anticipated aggression, or lifted high like a flag in excitement. A wagging tail does not indicate happiness so much as a targeted effort to remove a few pesky flies. A soft nicker obviously communicates a different message than the squeal of a stallion challenging another horse, but unlike a dog, whose bark and growl are readily expressive of his moods, a horse's vocalizations are usually more infrequent.

It also helps to study the horse's basic anatomy, if for no other reason than to know what is meant when the withers, loins, fetlock joints, pasterns, hocks, and other such parts of the horse are mentioned. In addition, the next time you observe a horse in action or standing still, whether a real horse or a visual depiction, try looking at him through new eyes, such as the eyes of the Hindu poet of the Upanishads who saw his entire world echoed in the horse's body. You can sense the mythic role of the horse in the lives of these earliest tamers of horses, as the horse's body symbolizes the vital forces of their world:

> The head is the dawn, its eye the sun, its vital breath the wind, its open mouth fire, and the trunk is the year. The back is heaven, the belly the intermediate region, the hoof the earth, the sides the four quarters, the ribs the intermediate quarters, the limbs the seasons, the joints the months and half months, the feet the days and nights, the bones the stars, the flesh the clouds. Its half-digested food is the sand, the blood vessels the rivers, the liver and lungs the mountains, the hair the herbs and trees. The forepart of the horse is the rising sun, and the hinder part the setting sun. Its yawn is lightning, its shaking of the body is thunder, its water is rain, and its neighing is indeed voice.[2]

It would help to investigate the many books on horses' herd behavior and their instinctual way of being in the world. For now, let's attune and sharpen our ways of perceiving our experiences with horses, understanding that their subtler expressiveness is based on their own highly attuned sensing and herd instincts. They respond to subtle energetic shifts in us also, as they would to others in their herd; in exploring this relationship, we have the opportunity to become more knowledgeable about sensitive communication. We can benefit from that subtle communication as horses carry us into our own mythic lives.

TRY THIS
Lean on Me: Fine-Tuning the Senses

More fully awakening our senses is a first step in working effectively with a horse. In fact, it is a good practice for anything we do, to do it in a mindful and fully present state, for safety as well as greater enjoyment. I believe that the reason most people turn to drugs or other addictions is that they are looking for deeper engagement in their lives. Through drugs, their dull lives suddenly seem to them to be brighter and better, with a sense of fascination and wonder. This activity with horses is the first of many that will naturally help open up brain and mind functions to one's wider life, so that artificial means are no longer needed. This activity assumes that you already know how to safely groom and lead a horse.

GOALS

- Fine-tune the senses by exploring your varied responses to inanimate and animate surroundings.
- Lay the foundation for understanding sensitive, energetic, nonverbal communication between sentient beings.
- Practice paying attention to the horse's basic modes of expression and communication.
- Practice respectful, safe, basic ways of handling horses.

PREPARATION AND EQUIPMENT

- One horse in halter with lead rope
- Grooming kit

- A few arena obstacles set out in the arena, for example, six to eight cones set up in a straight line, eight paces apart; several parallel ground poles; or a cavaletti or two

Time: Approximately one hour

Without your horse, lean against a solid wall somewhere in the barn area in a variety of ways — with your back, sides, and chest. As you do so, reflect on the following:

Notice how this surface feels to you: Is it cold or warm? Is it completely rigid or slightly flexible? Touch it with your fingers; is it rough or smooth?

What does it smell like? Go ahead; lean over and take a good whiff.

What kinds of feelings do you associate with the texture and feel of the wall?

Try knocking against the wall; how would you describe the sound?

What does this wall, or your leaning against it, remind you of?

If possible find a friend and ask permission to do the following exercise: lean against each other, back to back. The important task here is to notice the difference between your response to the wall and to a person. It's no longer a rigid surface. There's an element of trust that comes into play that you didn't have before.

Notice your feelings. Are you tempted to giggle or pull back? Do you feel cautious? A whole new set of feelings comes into play here. Try to describe them to yourself. You may feel pleasure, shyness, hesitance, or a mixture of many feelings.

Now, lean shoulder to shoulder. Check out with yourself if that feels different from the back-to-back position. (Notice that knocking this surface is no longer appropriate!) Compare this surface with the wall.

Now you are going to approach your horse with these same kinds of questions in mind. It is important to take an attitude of asking the horse's permission to approach and touch him. You can do this mentally as you approach the horse: "May I approach you now?" Keep the horse's name in mind too. You can say softly as you approach, "Hey there, Madison," or something to that effect. Running up to a horse would frighten him and evoke a flight response, as would any sudden movement. Horses will sense your attitude regardless of what it is, even if you are hiding it with your words. They can sometimes seem psychic that way. They are actually picking up subtle energetic cues from the way you express yourself, and you can learn to understand this kind of communication from them. For now, just try to observe signals from their ears, eyes, tails, and other body movements when they first notice you approaching.

As you approach, don't go right up and touch the nose or face. Imagine if someone did that to you. For many horses, that gesture feels invasive. The horse may reach toward you with his nose, because horses like to get acquainted with other horses by breathing into one another's nostrils. If your horse reaches out to you with his nose, you can try it if you wish; breathe into his nostrils without touching his face. Then approach the horse's shoulder, and if the horse seems at ease with your presence, go ahead and stroke his shoulder, all the while maintaining that attitude of asking permission. Notice for yourself the ways the horse acknowledges you. Did his ears point toward you, and if so, from how far away? Did his head rise higher, his eyes open wider? Did he step nervously aside or stand stock still? Each horse will respond differently. Just notice what you see and feel, without the need to interpret any meaning or guess at what feelings the horse's behavior indicates, unless of course you are being asked to move back and away.

After spending a few minutes meeting your horse, carefully, with an attitude of asking permission, first put your hand on the horse's shoulder, then gently turn your shoulder and lean into the horse, if that feels like a safe thing to do.

Engage your senses once again, as you did a few minutes ago with the wall and with your human partner.

What are your eyes and ears telling you? Take a deep whiff of the horse's hair and skin. How does it feel, physically and emotionally, to be shoulder to shoulder with your horse, to be this close to such a big animal, however gentle?

It may feel good or it may feel risky. Is your heart pounding? Notice how your body responds to this experience. Where do you feel various sensations — in your belly, chest, ears, head, or elsewhere?

Stand back for a moment, close your eyes, and scan your body. Start at the top of your head and move your attention down through your head, shoulders and upper back, chest, heart, stomach and other internal organs, intestines, hips, thighs, lower legs, and feet. What do you notice? Is there tightness anywhere in your body? Are there feelings of hot or cold? Just take note for now. When you do this, you practice mindfulness, emptying your mind of extraneous thoughts as you attend only to your body. As thoughts intrude about other things, such as your plans for later today, a conversation you've just had — anything, really — just set them aside and turn your attention back to your body and its sensations.

Now open your eyes and thank your horse. Then take a brush and currycomb, and begin grooming your horse with the same attentive attitude to both your own and your horse's reactions. When you have completed the basic grooming, lead the horse through a variety of obstacles on the ground, all the while practicing the same attention as previously.

After a few minutes, lead the horse to his stall or pasture and take a few minutes to notice what information and reflections this fine-tuning of your senses has revealed to you.

IN OUR WESTERN CULTURE we tend to communicate primarily with words, but we have a whole palette of other tools that comes into play when we begin to ride a horse. We communicate most obviously at the physical level, with our legs directing the horse's speed and direction, with subtle shifts of our weight in the saddle, and with tugs from our hands on the reins. Our voice plays a relatively small role compared to these other riding aids, although horses do learn simple commands and most certainly understand our tone of voice. And as with Madison, the horse who joined our circled group, we find that horses often understand more than we realize.

Another horse, named Dually, taught me the importance of using language more frequently. Trained as a cutting horse, this highly sensitive horse was donated to our therapeutic-riding herd due to recurrent lameness, which we felt would not arise again, considering the level of work in our program. However, after several weeks, Dually's nervousness caused me to question whether he would be suitable for our work. I surmised that he had experienced some kind of emotional trauma earlier in his life; his current owner had only recently acquired him and knew little of his past. One of our volunteers had learned of an animal communicator who had recently moved to our community. She offered to arrange for a session with her for Dually.

One of the results of the session was that the animal communicator advised me to tell Dually in detail each day why we needed him in the program and exactly what each of our students needed from him. This was a considerable departure from our normal routine, but I was willing to give it a try. Sure enough, when I explained to Dually each day which student he would work with and what he could offer that student, the lessons improved significantly. I spent three or four minutes at first, and less time after a few days, telling him the name of the student and the relevant issues, what we planned to work on that day, and how I hoped he could help.

One day, after a few weeks of this new routine, I was preoccupied with a parent who needed to talk to me, and I did not take the time for my usual conversation with Dually. That day he was clearly out of sorts, which confirmed for me the importance of our "talks." After that, I made a point of taking the time, if even for a few seconds, to review the day's schedule with him, and Dually grew in confidence. It was a remarkably simple solution that was confirmed in its effectiveness every time I failed to take the time for it. Although I can't say such a tactic elicits visible effects on every horse, I can say that it has worked more often than I would have dreamed. I talk to horses a lot more now than I used to.

ONE CALL TO ADVENTURE was created by Jean Auel in *The Valley of the Horses.* Fictional stories like this one, which show the power inherent in our partnership and communication with horses, draw their dramatic force from the mythic elements that they embody. When we listen deeply to such stories as these, even reading them aloud with animation and drama, they can call forth our own mythic stories and provide opportunities for seeding profound and positive change in our lives. These stories become more fertile for our lives when we participate in related activities designed to give us experiential grounding of their importance for us. We can more deeply anchor their wisdom through our bodies and allow their transformational power to be fully realized. The story of Ayla offers such an opportunity:

Ayla was a young woman living in prehistoric times. As a young child, she was rescued by a Neolithic tribe of human predecessors called the Clan of the Cave Bear. This community taught her many new skills that were foreign to her family's tribe, such as how to listen to plants to know their nutritional and healing values, and how to enter deeper states of consciousness for other knowledge. They communicated with hand and arm gestures and rudimentary sounds, instead of the language that Ayla recalled from her own human tribe, whose pale skin and hair contrasted with the more gorilla-like appearance of the Clan. When Ayla was a young woman, the tribe eventually ostracized her when they discovered her secretly practicing the men's hunting skills.

Living alone in a valley, she began securing food and shelter for the winter. In doing so, she trapped and killed a young mare, a traditional source of food in her world. She then discovered the mare's young filly hovering around, seeking her mother. Eager for the companionship, Ayla took the little one into her cave and fed her for the winter. In an early passage from the story, spring had arrived, and Ayla had taught the filly, named Whinney, to come running whenever she pursed her lips and whistled like the birds she had heard recently. Ayla began to hear a call to adventure that led her in an entirely new direction. "I wish I could run like you do," she thought. "Then we could both run together wherever we wanted . . . wouldn't it be wonderful if I could run like her." For some time she was preoccupied with the idea of running with the horse. "Then an idea struck her. Such an idea would not have occurred to her if she hadn't lived with the animal all winter, thinking of her as a friend and companion. And certainly she would not have acted on such a thought if she were still living with the Clan. But Ayla had become more used to following her impulses."[3] Before long, the young woman found a way to slip onto the filly's back, and though Whinney pranced nervously and backed her ears, she trusted the woman who had fed and sheltered her for the past year. The filly tried to run away from the weight on her back at first but was tired after a short run and stopped, with her sides heaving.

> The ride was a thrill she could hardly contain. The very idea of going along with a horse when it galloped filled Ayla with a sense of wonder. She had never dreamed such a thing was possible. No one had.
>
> Ayla could hardly keep herself off the horse's back. Riding the young mare as she galloped at top speed was an inexpressible joy. It thrilled her more than anything she had ever known. Whinney seemed to enjoy it as well, and she quickly became accustomed to carrying the woman on her back. The valley soon became too small to contain the woman and her galloping steed. They often raced across the steppes east of the river, which were easy to reach.[4]

Initially Ayla rode passively, letting the horse take her wherever she chose. Soon Ayla began to notice the play of the horse's muscles, and Whinney noticed Ayla's tension and relaxation. They already had established a desire to please each other. Eventually the continuous riding developed a more sensitive relationship between the two. "Whinney's reactions came to be so finely tuned that Ayla had only to think of where she wanted to go and at what speed and, as though the animal were an extension of her own body, the horse responded. The young woman didn't realize she had transmitted signals through nerves and muscles to the highly sensitive skin of her mount."[5]

The partnership that these two developed was the result of innate differences between horse and human, instead of any conscious attempt at training.

> Horses were social animals, normally living in herds, and they needed the closeness and warmth of fellow creatures. The sense of touch was particularly developed and important in establishing close rapport. But the young mare's instincts led her to follow directions, to go where she was led.
>
> The woman's actions had purpose, were directed by a brain in which foresight and analysis were constantly interacting with knowledge and experience. Her vulnerable position kept her survival reflexes sharp and forced her to be constantly aware of her surroundings, which together had precipitated and accelerated the training process. The sight of a hare or giant hamster, even while she was riding for pleasure, tended to make Ayla reach for her sling and want to go after it. Whinney had quickly interpreted her desire, and her first step in that direction led ultimately to the young woman's tight, though unconscious, control of the horse.[6]

You may feel that you have never experienced quite such a revolutionary and original idea that served as a call to a new adventure as Ayla does in this story, but you can be fairly certain that your reason for reading this book, or your desire to be around horses, springs from a similar call. You can experiment with the kind of sensitive communication that Ayla developed while living with Whinney in her own dwelling. Here is an activity to help you begin to learn the kind of close communication in which you seemingly have only to think of what you'd like to do with your horse, and as if the horse were an extension of your own body, he responds.

TRY THIS
Listening to Your Body: Exploring Your Energetic Communication with a Horse

In addition to responding to the overt use of your hands, legs, voice, and weight aids, horses also respond to more subtle messages from you at the psychological level. These relate to your moods, subtext, or thoughts occurring in their presence, and the energetic approach you take to them. I often have arrived to exercise a horse, found the ride not going well, and then realized that I had ignored a headache or thought about the implications of a recent meeting while interacting with the horse. The energy and attention behind my words, gestures, and actions made the difference, and the horse sensed and reflected the dissonance. You can develop your skills with these subtle forms of energy so that they become an important tool in many human interactions. Paying attention to your own awareness of subtle cues from others can give you information for negotiating complex interactions and for better understanding the underlying messages in ordinary conversations. You find that you have a much larger palette of information for all your communications. Here is an activity to begin working with a horse toward that end, as did Ayla in the story above, so that you can attune to subtle communication between you and your horse, and explore new adventures for you both.

GOALS
- Gain greater awareness of subtle cues and information from your body.

- Learn how body language is an important and effective tool for communication and leadership.
- Lay the groundwork for energy healing work.

PREPARATION AND EQUIPMENT

- Round pen, small riding area, or paddock
- Mature horse that is trustworthy to respond without aggression toward inexperienced people

Time: Thirty to sixty minutes

Lead an experienced and trusted horse into a round pen or other similar midsize area. Step out of the pen for a moment to prepare for the activity. You will later reenter the pen and spend some time with the horse, asking the horse to walk with you, move away, or anything that feels appropriate and also stays within the parameters of safety and mutual respect.

Before beginning, briefly review safety guidelines, as well as the importance of taking a nonverbal stance of requesting the horse's permission throughout, even when asserting leadership.

Before entering the pen with the horse, turn away from the round pen and the horse, and mentally scan your body. Focus as you did in this chapter's previous activity, "Lean on Me," when you moved your attention down your body, from head to toe, noticing any physical sensations without interpreting them. If there is a twitch in one knee or the stomach, at this point you just want to notice it, without speculating on the significance of these sensations.

Next, opening your eyes, turn and enter the round pen, and interact with the horse for the next five minutes however you wish, as long as safety is maintained.

Many variations occur at this point. Some people will simply stand a distance away from the horse. Others will approach, stroke the horse, and encourage the horse to walk with them, with varying levels of success. Some take on a commanding manner and become very focused on having the horse move forward, which the horse may or may not respond to. Others are not interested in commanding. They may wish only to stroke the horse and get acquainted.

After you have spent five minutes with the horse, take some time to reflect, perhaps in a journal, on what you notice in your body now, how you feel about the experience, what it reminds you of, and what surprised or challenged you.

THIS SEEMINGLY SIMPLE ACTIVITY can offer interesting and powerful experiences. For instance, the first time I personally did this activity, I entered the pen with a horse that was new to me, who had just previously stood afar from another woman during her time in the pen with him. She related later that she had sensed the horse quietly inviting her to approach. She had walked to his side and touched his back as he continued to stand quietly.

Just a few minutes later, I stood at the gate to the pen and scanned my body, noticing only a slight twinge in one knee. However, when I turned to enter the pen, the horse quickly moved toward me and stood so close to the gate that I had to squeeze through to get inside. He immediately began to nuzzle my shoulder and chest. I was taken aback by this markedly different, but friendly, behavior from a horse I had never met. I stepped away from him, only to have him follow me, clearly wanting to continue the nuzzling. My astonishment quickly gave way to tears, as I felt my heart opening in a way that had me totally nonplussed. I began to stroke the horse's ears and neck, and then moved to his side. As long as I continued to touch him, he was content. If I stepped away, he turned and approached me. He seemed to crave a connection with me that I could not help but return. After decades of working with horses, I was used to this kind of affection from familiar horses. But this horse was a stranger who was able to crack open wide the feelings of joy and wonder I had missed during an overwhelmingly stressful time in my life. I felt a renewed trust in life, as though a special blessing had been bestowed upon me.

AS A FOLLOW-UP TO THIS EXERCISE, you can explore a more energetic communication in which you take an active leadership role with the horse. This should be undertaken only with the help of an instructor or other experienced horse person. A horse will move away from a person giving energetic hand and voice signals for performing a walk, trot, canter, halt, and reverse directions. The same signals given with no real intention of the horse responding accomplishes just that — nothing. The horse will stand unresponsive or respond in confusion. Only focused, coherent, total body communication will accomplish the results of moving the horse calmly along the rail of the round pen, varying his gait as requested. All kinds of personal issues can intervene to distract one's focus and create a dissonance that a horse will notice and respond to.

Learning to communicate from a distance with more than voice provides a major challenge for most people. You may be used to relying on language to communicate with people or on equipment like a halter and lead rope to communicate with a horse. Most people are unaware of the implications of their level of focus, emotional state, body posture, and body language. When you begin to take leadership with a horse, you have the opportunity to utilize these aspects of yourself and try new ways of communicating with a horse, a being who is responsive to your subtle cues of body language and emotional states. It can give you a real taste of your personal potential for a larger palette of communication skills for other situations.

One way to explore new areas of body language is to play with the difference between imitation and mimesis. Actors intimately know the difference between the two. Imitation relegates performance to repeating a character's lines, donning a costume, and walking about a stage. Such a performance is more suited for Halloween parades or costume parties. Mimesis, on the other hand, is when actors find that part within themselves that is aligned with the character — when they know the character's feelings as their own and seek through introspection and research some part of themselves that can identify with the character's story. Then their performance has the ring of truth to it, a coherence that comes of having done their human homework with the role.

This was a helpful lesson for a friend who had worked for many years with horses. Julie was working with her own very exuberant young horse who ran about the arena giving her little or no attention. She was intimidated by the horse's behavior and was repeatedly unsuccessful in commanding his attention, even though she had owned the horse for over two years. Her trainer suggested that she get his attention by taking on a more aggressive stance by acting like a cat, a natural predator of a horse. At first, Julie was clearly pretending in a rather unconvincing way, raising one arm and snarling with a grin on her face. The horse responded to her underlying intimidation by continuing his running about. Her trainer suggested she needed to get into her own "cat-ness," her own feline nature, so to speak, to imagine what it would feel like to have claws and to snarl and leap gracefully and powerfully onto the back of a horse. She suggested that she close her eyes and find that place within herself. After a moment, she opened her eyes, raised her hands, curled her fingers and crouched and let out a loud shout that was as close as she could get to a snarl. She stepped into mimesis instead of just imitating a cat, discovered in her body her own "cat-ness." Her horse immediately slid to a stop, squarely facing her with a snort of curiosity and astonishment. With this imaginative role-playing, Julie found her way into another part of herself that could be assertive in the face of her horse's overwhelming exuberance. With a few reassuring words, she was able to approach her horse with his full attention. Interestingly, she later discovered a new way to step into needed assertiveness in a difficult relationship with her boyfriend.

You may find it helpful to invigorate your communication with your horse by taking on the role of another animal or person for a few moments, one who represents a calm and assertive energy. The purpose is not to intimidate the horse but to raise your assertiveness to a level that it will enlist the horse's attention and cooperation. If you are too aggressive with a horse, the horse will respond in fear or defensiveness. It is important in this situation, of course, to pay attention, back off, and to reflect on a more effective way to communicate with the horse, one that will enlist cooperative partnership.

WITH THESE SIMPLE BUT POTENT ACTIVITIES, you can start to explore the subtle tools that become available when you listen to your body. If you are inexperienced, when you explore these aspects of interaction between yourself and a horse, it is important to do so either with the guidance of an instructor or another experienced horse person. Once you can rest assured that the horse has a basic relationship of trust, you can enjoy exploring the possibilities for yourself and your horse by embarking on a new adventure that will have far-reaching benefits for you both. You are building a foundation for further work that will carry you into your mythic life.

CHAPTER FOUR

ALLIES FOR THE JOURNEY

Activating Aspects of the Self through Your Imaginal Body

FOR OUR MYTHIC LIVES, horses are just as important in their role as inner allies populating our imaginations as they are when acting as outer partners in physical form. This is especially true for those of us who are not able to own a horse. But whether or not a person can access a live horse, a rich and explored inner life of the imagination provides a critically important stage upon which to live the theater of one's mythic life. In a world where the predominance of television and movies often compromises our imaginative skills by making us passive viewers, it has become important to attend to our underdeveloped imaginations so that we may enlist our inner allies. Developing our imaginative skills can help us activate important aspects of ourselves, bringing into play fuller functioning of our brains and bodies.

Competitive sports have harnessed this power by developing mental exercises for athletes that use the mind to enable maximum physical performance. When I worked with competitive horse-show students, we often rehearsed mentally the perfect performance. The more they were able to vividly imagine the details of what it took to have the perfect ride, the better those details were integrated into their actual, physical performances. If they were not visually inclined, they were encouraged to use their other senses while developing the less-active visual senses — to hear or even smell what the perfect ride might be. It was a nightly practice for them to seed their dreams with this imaginative rehearsal. In addition, it was equally important to imagine all their worst fears of what could go wrong and then how they would deal with these situations — whom they might call on for help, how they might ease the horse out of a situation when the animal shied away from a flapping flag or was caught next to another out-of-control horse, how they might maintain calm by slowing their breathing when under the judge's scrutiny, what attitude they wished to cultivate for the times when a problematic ride resulted in no ribbon at all. Students could easily transfer this mindful practice to other challenges in their schoolwork and personal lives.

This conscious inner work provides many more benefits. You are building an interior landscape of your own that can yield far-reaching benefits for your outer world. When you populate your imaginal life with vivid images of characters you have chosen to accompany and empower you as allies, that power goes with you into all of your daily situations.

This understanding may seem to contradict what you were told in the past: "Stop daydreaming." "Attend to the real situation." "You're off in your fantasy world again." These are familiar phrases intended to encourage us to focus and attend fully to the tasks at hand. And certainly, escaping into a fantasy world can be hazardous. However, attending only to the practical, the tangible, and the real world denies us access to the vast resources of our brain-mind system. We can harness those resources when we explore the power of the imaginal world, the realms of the mythic self that lie within and without. When we explore and enhance these realms, we find that we bring more of ourselves to those tasks that well-meaning teachers and parents want us to accomplish. We find that our effectiveness in the outer world can dramatically take us into directions we never dreamed possible before.

We dwell in much more than our tangible flesh-and-blood world. In many societies, our bodies are recognized as one visible layer of many other layers that extend invisibly out from our physical forms, as demonstrated in the chakra system and the energy meridians of Chinese medicine. Our subtle bodies interact with those of others without even physically touching them. These subtle bodies resonate with energy. We have all experienced these energy bodies whenever we've noticed a charismatic figure enter a room. Horses are extremely sensitive to this subtle energy, as we noticed and explored with the activity "Lean on Me" in chapter 3. When we activate and heighten our five senses, we become more attuned to the sensing of our subtle bodies, and with some practice, especially with our horse partners, we can develop greater capacities for communication skills of all kinds.

As a result of an impoverished acquaintance with this imaginal aspect of themselves, people often turn to various addictions. When one explores the power of the imaginal world, the yearning previously answered with addictive substances is instead harnessed for its promise. We recognize the yearning as our innermost self calling us to our fully realized life, the divine seed within each of us that seeks to grow into its full form.

In an initial approach to developing our imaginal lives, we can first simply focus on memories that emerge in the midst of the trying situations characteristic of any hero's journey. At these challenging times, memories can become gold mines, yielding wisdom for current life scenarios. When a memory of a horse, whether fictional or not, springs to mind in a current situation, you can trust that it has come to offer insight. Exploring that memory for its relevance, especially when it may seem quite unrelated to your circumstances, can lead to enlightening realizations. In his book *Bio-Spirituality: Focusing as a Way to Grow*, Peter A. Campbell tells this story of a childhood memory that helped him deal with an overwhelming situation in midlife, when a back injury and subsequent depression catapulted him into a short-lived hero's journey. Seeking guidance, he decided to "walk the inner road":

> The image which eventually came surprised me. It was far more profound than I realized at first. As a youngster I had, for health reasons, attended a boarding school in the Arizona desert. It was an isolated little ranch about twenty miles from Tucson. Horseback riding was available, and I soon fell in love with getting out on a mount and riding for miles through the desert.
>
> We were not allowed to do this alone, of course. But one morning at dawn, when I was only seven years old, I used the watering trough to stand on and saddled up alone before any staff or children were stirring. Then I rode straight out into the sunrise. It was a glorious day and I explored the desert for an hour or more, giving little thought to anything except what lay ahead of me. At some point it dawned on me to get my bearings, and I turned to check for familiar landmarks. But the surrounding arroyos gave no hint of a direction home. There were no familiar markers. Just sagebrush, cactus, and an unending series of little hills that all looked the same. I realized with a sudden chill that I was lost.
>
> Searching for a while, I desperately tried to find my way home, but I soon realized it was hopeless. I remember my inner panic and growing sense of isolation — much like feelings that would come later in life whenever fear or confusion would overtake me. Only gradually did my attention return to my horse, who was peacefully waiting for me to signal with reins and stirrups where we were to go next.
>
> At that point I was inspired to do one of the few sensible things a youngster in my predicament could do. I stopped trying to figure things out for myself and made what may have been one of the first consciously deliberate acts of trust in my young life. I knew I was lost, but deep down I felt that the horse knew his way home.

The remembered experience of how I deliberately lifted the reins and let them drop on the horse's neck somehow fit what my body knew about pain and confusion as I focused forty years later. It had not been forgotten.

There had been a deliberate letting go and trusting out there in the desert years before. It was a letting go of everything that wanted to control the situation, a kind of abandonment to some wisdom that lay beyond anything I could muster within myself.

That morning, among the sagebrush and cacti, the horse's first response to my loosening of the reins was to begin nibbling the sparse grass at his feet. Unaccustomed to such lack of direction, he stood still for a while, looking about before he moved on to get more grass.

I remember how hard it was to resist the temptation to move him about. I desperately wanted to reassert my control, holding the reins, guiding him now one way, now another. But my feeling, even as a child, was that he had to experience a sense of himself as boss if we were ever to get home before nightfall. And so I waited ... and waited ... and waited. It seemed endless.

Finally I noticed the horse stretching his neck, stretching his head, and testing the looseness of the reins. Instead of grazing haphazardly, he began to move in a definite direction. Snatching mouthfuls of grass, he would move on a few paces before reaching for another tuft as we passed.

Gradually the stops became less frequent, his pace quickened, and eventually he broke into a trot, with only occasional questioning looks over his shoulder, and then a determined, careening gallop. It was a wild ride home. I narrowly missed the outstretched spines of cholla cactus and barely grazed the giant saguaro so plentiful in that part of the desert. Terrified, I clutched the saddle horn, torn between a desperate desire to rein in this lurching juggernaut and the equally strong fear that if I did we might never get home.

Finally, familiar landmarks appeared. We slowed, stopped, and rested a bit. I even imagined a mischievous glint in the equine eye as he turned to see how I was doing.

The rest of the return was uneventful. Little did I then realize that the personal significance of this event would lie dormant in me for almost forty years before coming back to teach me more about myself.

I learned through this that the way home is written deep within each of us. Somewhere beneath all of our daily "reacting" — getting jobs done, meals prepared, bills paid, and all our survival planning — lies a realm of deeper meaning, purpose, and direction. The horse, as I have found, is really a largely unowned aspect of ourselves. There is something within each of us that knows the real meaning of human life. At certain times it can break through the shallow awareness that fills most of our waking moments.[1]

For many of us, our fast-paced lives have eclipsed this kind of exploration of our own imaginations. Cell phone conversations and plans for the next meeting or activity often occupy our long commutes. Cable networks and large-screen televisions sometimes occupy every major room in a home with ongoing sound and images. We've lost contact with the inner allies who reside within our bodily knowing. The following activity is designed to bring your attention back to your own muscular imagination and give you powerful tools for enlisting your imaginal body for your own mythic journey, allowing you to get acquainted with a wide array of inner allies. This activity is based on similar exercises by Jean Houston.

TRY THIS
Developing Your Imaginal Body

Developing skills with your imagination through your imaginal body brings you many gifts to take along on your journey.[2] Think of the imaginal body as a muscular imagination, a vivid, detailed imagining of the body in movement. You can develop an acute sense of this muscular imagination, and it can nurture your talents for learning deeply, performing more effectively, and returning your trust in your own bodily knowing. It can enhance your ability to partner with your horse. It can introduce you to important inner allies. This bodily knowing gives you access to increased information for all kinds of decision making. Even more, it is one of the most important tools for developing your compassion for others and for discerning accurately how to respond wisely to their needs. You can use your imaginal body to learn things you normally could not do, such as athletic feats. And you can use it to heal, travel, imagine, create, and enter into the sensibilities of other people and animals.

GOALS
- Begin to develop an awareness of the imaginal body as a tool for greater effectiveness in your life.
- Practice compassion by entering into the sensibilities of other animals.

PREPARATION AND EQUIPMENT

This activity can be done individually or in a group. As a group activity it requires a leader who will read the script below. As an individual, you can make an audio recording of the script and use the recording to guide you through the exercise. Pause between steps when it seems appropriate; the most important pauses are indicated in the script. For this activity, you will need the following:

- A chair for each person
- Space for participants to move around near the place where they are sitting, indoors or outdoors

(No horses are required for this activity.)
Time: Forty-five minutes

EXPLORING THE IMAGINAL BODY
Stand with your knees relaxed and your eyes closed. Focus on your breathing as a way of directing your attention inward. Make sure that your weight is evenly balanced between both of your feet and stand in a relaxed position.

As you remain standing, reach as high as you can with your right arm. Feel all the muscles in your arm, hand, and fingers as you stretch.

Now lower your arm. Feel what it's like to relax all those muscles, how the blood drops down into your arm and fingers.

Repeat the raising and lowering of your arm several times, remaining conscious of the full sensation in your body.

Now *imagine* raising your right arm. Try to experience this as vividly as you did when you physically raised your real arm. Imagine lowering your right arm. You are now using your muscular imagination, or your imaginal body.

Raise and lower your real arm. Then raise and lower your imaginal arm. Go back and forth between your real and imaginal arms a number of times, and then go through the same process with your left arm. Remember to experience your imaginal arms with as much awareness as when you stretch your real arms.

Now, with your real body, pretend that you are sword fighting and make a lunge to the right. Feel all the muscles and nerves in your arm, back, and legs. Then come back to center.

Now, this time with your imaginal body, make another lunge. Feel all those muscles and nerves in your imaginal arm, imaginal chest and sides, and imaginal legs, and then come back to center.

Alternating between the physical and imaginal bodies, lunge to the right several more times, returning to center each time.

Lunge with your real body to the left, then with your imaginal body. Repeat this a few times.

Pay careful attention to the next instruction.

Lunge with your imaginal body to the right and, at the same time, lunge to the left with your real body. Keep your attention on your imaginal body. Come back to center.

Lunge with your real body to the right at the same time your imaginal body lunges to the left. Come back to center.

Be aware of the space in front of you. Jump with your real body into that space. Now jump back. Repeat this a number of times.

Now, with your imaginal body, jump forward and back several times.

Imagine that standing before you in your imaginal body is your ideal, but possible, body image. It may be stronger, slimmer, larger, more flexible, or whatever is important to you. Actually feel this image in front of you. Hold the image very strongly of this ideal, but possible, imaginal body in front of you. Research has proven that when you can hold somewhat consistently a better body image in your mind, your physical body begins to improve accordingly.

With your real body, jump forward *into* this ideal, but possible, imaginal body, so that there is a merging between your real body and your imaginal body.

Open your eyes and walk around the room in your ideal body and your real body. Notice how you feel.

ENTERING THE SENSIBILITIES OF ANIMALS

Go back and sit down. Make yourself comfortable. Close your eyes. Focus on your breathing: in and out in a regular and relaxed way. Keeping your eyes closed, have a sense that you're breathing through the very center of your actual body. Breathe very deeply so that you get a sense of your breath being pulled up through the middle as you inhale, and pulled down through the middle as you exhale.

Imagine your body lying on the floor in front of you in a comfortable position, arms to your sides, feet about twelve inches apart. Feel the surface beneath your body, hands, and arms. Feel the floor.

Now place your left imaginal hand on your chest, with its elbow out at shoulder height. Raise your imaginal elbow toward the sky, flapping your arm like the wing of a bird. Flap it up and down.

Now put your right imaginal hand also on your chest and perform the same movement, so that both arms flap up and down like a bird.

Think of the bird flapping its wings. Think about the muscular wing-bone structure of the bird as you flap your arms.

As you continue to flap your imaginal arms, discover that your body is now the body of a bird. Flapping your strong wings, you are a great bird soaring through the heavens. Feel your wings flapping, and your body soaring in the sky. Enjoy the feeling of strength and the great cushion of air as you flap your wings, as your body soars on the wind currents. Look down with incredible precision and vision at the land beneath you. Do you see that tasty worm down there a thousand feet below? Swoop down and get it! You see that high tree? Perch on one of its highest branches and look at the landscape around you. Stay alert. Stay awake. Stay focused. Stay in the body of the imaginal bird. Now fly off again. Soar and glide. Enjoy the marvelous experience of flying as a bird. (Pause for about thirty seconds.)

Cease this imaginal movement. Exit the body of the bird and let your consciousness hang suspended without form.

Now find yourself in the body of a large cat — a tiger, lion, leopard, cheetah, or panther — whatever you wish. Move in this wonderful, supple, graceful, lithe, powerful body of a great cat. Be aware of the tremendous power and grace of this body you are now in. Make a great leap to a high rock! Bound across a plain. Climb up a mighty tree.

Feel the strength in your claws and hindquarters, your muscular hindquarters with their great swooping powerful muscular tail, as you pull yourself up.

Growl loudly and feel the vibration of your sound in the very tree on which you stand. Look out at the world through the eyes of this great cat. Feel its pleasure in its body. Feel its consciousness. (Pause.)

Lose that body. Let your consciousness hang suspended.

Now find yourself in the body of a great snake. Feel that body as it undulates and slithers along the earth, with its tongue darting in and out of its mouth.

How do you sense the earth as you undulate, wriggle, and slide? Sensuously feel every stone, every crevice, every blade of grass

against your skin, as your slick body slides along, experiencing subtle vibrations in the air and the earth. Slide along the earth, but stay
awake, stay alert. You're a snake. Look out at the world from snake
consciousness.You have the wisdom of the serpent, as well as the
body — knowledge of earth, cycles, and seasons.

Lose that body. Let your consciousness hang suspended once
again.

Transfer your consciousness into the body of a dolphin.

Be in the dolphin with a great school of dolphins, talking to
each other in high-pitched sonic song. You are rolling, leaping, and
playing.

You see a great group of sharks, your natural enemies. Fearless
and dutiful, go over and bump the sharks away with your powerful
head. Now go back to playing and rolling.

Understand the subtle communication among dolphins. Know
what it is to be a dolphin and to have its great wisdom, since it has
been so bright, so intelligent in the sea some 25 million years.
(Pause.)

Lose that body. Let your consciousness hang suspended.

Now find yourself in the body of a horse. Perhaps it is a horse you
have ridden recently. Perhaps it is another whose beauty and movement have captured your attention.

Notice the shiny color of your coat — red, black, or spotted — as
you stand in the spring grass of a pasture that stretches for acres
and acres.

Enjoy a gallop through the pasture, mane flowing, head tossing.
Feel your hooves pound the ground. Hear the thunder of your whole
herd around you. They all slow down and trot, while you snort and
toss your head, glorying in the splendor of grass, sky, and clear sun-
shine.

You take a leap up in the air just for fun, and squeal as another
horse comes near to play. Your neck arches in greeting. You are a

creature of beauty and graceful movement, an inhabitant of the wide-open plains — you and your fellow horses of so many colors.

You walk to a nearby stream and lower your head, mane dropping to tickle your face as you take a long, cool drink. After the gallop, it tastes so sweet to your hot, sweaty body.

Now lose that horse body. Let your consciousness hang suspended.

MEETING YOUR HIGHER SELF

Still sitting in your real body with your eyes closed, be in your own imaginal body as it rises up and walks around the area or room. Sense very clearly its movements and sensations. See if it is now clearer to be in the imaginal body. Roll and run through the area here. Let your movement be lithe, agile, and free.

Now, pick a favorite, pleasurable place you'd like to visit, perhaps a mountain lake you can plunge into or a great restaurant where you can have a splendid meal, and go there in your imaginal body. Experience that place fully. (Pause.)

Now let only your imaginal body stand up. And as it does, let your highest self — your essential self with all its capacities in place, loaded with possibilities for your own unfolding — join with your imaginal body in its rich unfolding.

Stay alert. Stay awake. Your imaginal body is being filled with your essential self, filled with light, filled with your tremendous possibilities. It is the body of wholeness, of fulfillment. All of your dreams and hopes for yourself are fully developed in this body of the higher self. Even your lesser talents are fully realized and you are able to accomplish great deeds. Your high self is full of light, joy, and beauty, and is merging with your imaginal body.

Filled with your high self, let your imaginal body come over to you and sit opposite you. And let that imaginal body, sitting opposite you, reach into your mind and body to help effect physiological, emotional, and mental healing, and the quickening of all your possibilities.

Know that, working with your imaginal body, your high self has the fluidity to reach into your physical body to heal, forgive, or activate your highest capacities or evolutionary qualities — whatever is needed. Feel yourself being tuned, sharpened, quickened, perhaps even enlightened. With its sense of union with your high self, your imaginal body knows a great deal about what is appropriate for you. It is happening now. It is beautiful!

And now, in your imaginal body, filled with your high self, approach the animal body of a horse. Lightly leap onto the horse's back, no saddle or bridle needed. Your horse stands quietly and drops his head down in total relaxation.

For a few moments take the pose depicted in the great painting of the Indian on his pony, with your head raised to the sky, chest opened wide, arms falling to your sides, feathers streaming down your back from your headdress, spine arched slightly backward, legs extending relaxed down each side of your horse. You stand together atop a great mountain, overseeing vast and beautiful landscapes all around you, hills rolling into the horizon in layers of color, shades of green and purple. Having just felt that connection so intimately in your imaginal body's adventures, for a moment know your connection with the entire natural world. Feel deep gratitude for your horse, who holds you connected between heaven and earth.

Now in your physical body, open your eyes, get up, and stretch. Let the imaginal body either, through breathing, move into your physical body, or let it release itself to go and play with all the horses you've ever known.

Notice how you feel in your body. How do you feel about your engagement in your day-to-day life? Do you see what you can do? Did you feel yourself tuning your mind?

DISCUSSION

Now you know that you can get into the mind and soul of a horse or other animal and acquire some of its deep knowing, its generosity of spirit. You also can become the body and mind of your higher self.

When you go to bed tonight, get into your imaginal body and say to your upcoming dreams, "Tonight I am a horse." Become a horse and see what happens through your dreams. As you become conscious of the ability to orchestrate your body-mind systems, you will find a rich, new resource in your dreams. Perhaps ask your dream for a dream guide or guardian, or maybe an animal totem. See what emerges.

As you work more with a flesh-and-blood horse, you will find that harnessing the power of your imaginal body can give remarkable benefits. For instance, it can give you new tools for moving in greater synchrony with your horse's complex motion. When you ride at a walk, try directing your imaginal body to drop down a few inches into your horse's back, so that as your physical body rides on a saddle, your imaginal body rides bareback. With your spine directly aligned with your horse's spine, feel your flesh touch your horse's flesh, and experience the muscular movement directly on your skin so that your muscles respond to the horse's movement with immediacy and warmth. Then continue by vividly imagining that your legs are long enough to almost reach the ground, connecting you to the ground on which your horse walks. Once you feel the increased connection with your horse's movement at a walk, try it at a trot and a canter. Notice the increased fluidity of your movement. Often your horse will respond with more relaxed, fluid movement too.

DEVELOPING YOUR IMAGINAL BODY through this activity and others that follow provides you with the most important key to entering the realm of your mythic life. In future chapters, we will explore how to use your imaginal body to bring more comfort to your horse, as well as communicate more sincerely and effectively with your horse. These same techniques can be applied to interactions with people, so that you develop more options for responding with compassion and wisdom to stressful interactions and situations. They also give you access to your mythic companions, the broader community of characters who accompany you on your own hero's journey.

CHAPTER FIVE

ENERGY, COMMUNICATION, AND THE EXPANDED SELF

Developing Tools for Healing

THE BELLY OF THE WHALE in the hero's journey names those times
when we need to attend to and develop our inner lives. These are
times of quiet, sometimes involving long periods of disciplined work,
for gaining the inner tools needed for the rest of our journey, which
will require more outward action. The imaginal body is an important inner tool to develop during those times. As we become aware of
our imaginal bodies through the way of the horse, we take on skills
that enable exploring the art of subtle communication and delving
deeply to retool our psyches. We no longer need to rely only on words,
actions, or any particular communication skill. Instead we can allow
our communication to arise from a deeper place within. In this place,
we are aware of our ability to invisibly touch and be touched by those
around us. Our personal boundaries no longer stop at the interface of
our skin with the air around us. Our personal space becomes larger

and more potent than the three- or four-foot zone around us. When we observe and appreciate how a sensitive horse picks up on our presence at a distance, and how she responds to our body language and moods, we can recognize that the horse is leading us into a greater awareness of our own capabilities.

As our boundaries of awareness expand, we often discover that our lives are mirrored in those around us. We begin to see how there is a kind of dance between us and others in our lives. We have all been amused at how dog owners often resemble their doggy companions. One friend of mine, who enjoys bursts of spontaneity in her daily life, owns horses with a similar style in their joyful racing through winding trails. When looked at more carefully, this phenomenon can become a mind-bending exercise in understanding quantum realities.

Quantum physics has posited that these similarities are based on an atomic structure of the world more radical and fundamental than our conscious minds can initially comprehend. Even though quantum physics can seem like a scientific theory that no one really understands, including its originators, the practical applications of quantum physics are all around us. Were it not for quantum physics, common parts of our environment would not function: computers would not operate, power stations would not cool our homes, cell phones would not make calls, and our suppers would not warm on the stove.

Our customary view of the world assumes that phenomena are separated by time and space and that no influence on one part can travel faster than the speed of light to the other. Yet, in quantum theory, a paradox exists called *quantum nonlocality*. It states that two separate systems, spatially separated, have an instantaneous effect on each other. Quantum nonlocality proves that previous assumptions about separation of phenomena are incorrect, and that there is a holistic interconnectedness operating at the quantum level contradicting our familiar assumptions about our world. We seem to be immersed in a sea of interconnectivity. As a body of water connects ocean creatures, so the entire universe is interconnected in a kind of psychic sea. There is nothing that we are not attached to in some way. Rupert Sheldrake explains it this way: "Our intentions stretch out into the world around us, and also extend into the future. We are linked to our environment and to each other."[1] Regardless of what it is, what we hold in our minds has a powerful effect on the future. Our thoughts go forth and attract events, people, and things configured in response to those thoughts. We can see this in operation when we plan for the future. We may even make those plans especially concrete by creating pictures of them, by focusing our energy in visualizing the details. Before long, things happen, people show up, opportunities appear, and our lives begin to configure around those plans.

My friend Kate recently operated out of these quantum realities to address some important issues in her life. Following over four decades of experience with horses, she began to fear her Arabian mare, whom she had trained and ridden for five years. When ridden in a group of other horses, Kysis became very eager and assertive. She insisted on leading the group, sometimes becoming unmanageable when asked to travel behind other horses. At first Kate tried to ignore her fear, and continued working with her horse for months. Then one day they had an accident. As they rode up a steep hill behind two other horses, her horse slipped and fell down the hill, causing Kate to roll off into a tree and crack a rib. Over the next few months, she confronted the fact that she did not enjoy Kysis any longer, and traded her for another horse. Within a few weeks, she again traded this horse for another, then another. Each time, when the horse displayed some aggressive or unruly behavior, it triggered Kate's fear. She attributed the problems to each horse until she finally purchased a young horse with a quiet temperament. When this horse began to display the usual antics of any young horse, Kate again found herself reacting with fear. She knew that she had to look inward more seriously than she ever

had before. She suspected that her fear had caused the youthful behavior of the horse to escalate into something worse.

About this time, she heard that the new owner of one of her previous horses loved her quiet, reliable new mount. The new owner reported that the horse did not display any of the behavior that had
triggered Kate's fear. Kate decided that she had to look at how her own
fear contributed to the problems around her. Her horses mirrored her
own issues, rather than just displaying their own propensities for
aggressive behavior. She also knew that, because horses had been her
lifelong companions, they provided her with the playing ground for
resolving her fear. Sometimes it seemed like a cloud or fog had
descended on Kate, and she could not see out of it. She reflected on
how the fear had been a kind of underground issue for years. She came
to see that she held a story carried down through generations of her
family. She realized that the sudden death of her own daughter soon
after her granddaughter's birth a few years before, coupled with the
previous sudden death of two other young friends, had engendered a
general sense of foreboding about life. She began to feel that life could
not be trusted, that something bad always lurked, ready to bring pain
and sorrow. She sometimes found herself in physical pain when she
drove at night, as the dark triggered her underlying fear.

When she saw that other experiences in her life engendered her
fear and that fear factored in her larger story, Kate also knew that her
relationship with her horse could provide a path out of the fear. Selling this horse, or even completely turning her back on horses, was
clearly not a viable solution, even though previously, when she was
unaware of how she and her horse mirrored each other, it had seemed
a fine choice. Wisely, she sought a new trainer to give weekly lessons to
her and her young mare. She found a trainer who worked on the relationship with her horse instead of primarily on her horse's behavior.
Instead of focusing her horse's training on the usual behaviors of moving ahead over a stream crossing or responding readily to her cues for

walk, trot, canter, and other such issues, she began an exploration of the partnership with her horse that took into account the larger story within which they were engaged. She began to shift the story she was living, in which fear had been an unwelcome intruder to be ousted and her horse's misbehavior had seemed a call for discipline. Instead she anchored herself to the story of partnership with her horse, starting at the beginning, with basic ground training and arena work. She made the decision to shift away from the fear story into the partnership story. In this new story, when her fear arose in its usual unwelcome manner, she now had tools to approach it in a more effective way. Now, instead of contracting inside herself for protection, she looked outward to her horse to build partnership.

In doing so, Kate began to engage her imaginal body. She openly talked with her trainer and friends about her fear. She visualized the worst-possible scenario from the standpoint of her fear. She and her trainer sought tools for dealing with that possibility and avoiding dangerous situations. In these rehearsals she trained her imaginal body for new skills and deepened those she already had. From this vantage point of partnership, she realized that in the past when her body had held onto fear she had actually escalated her horse's fearful behavior. Her previous trainer had insisted that she take charge of the horse with an aggressive approach to the horse's refusals to obey. In the context of partnering with her horse, using her breath and the slightest movement of her hands and legs, Kate found simply requesting things in a subtle manner from her horse more effective.

The horse perceived these cues as something much more than simply a weaker signal. Instead, because of Kate's intention for partnership and her conversations and rehearsals with her trainer, her horse experienced signals from her imaginal body as well. Along with the story of partnership that Kate was creating for them both, her imaginal body's power backed up a slight pull on the rein. The horse responded eagerly to these startlingly subtle requests, going far beyond any performance goals Kate and her trainer had set previously. Now her horse did not refuse to move into a trot or canter, and did not panic when turning away from other horses. The previous resistance from her horse when asked for something new was met with Kate's subtle, firm, and reassuring requests instead of overt insistence on a certain behavior. Kate began to trust the partnership that her horse now mirrored. In turn, her horse grew to trust that partnership as well. In using her imaginal body for this purpose, Kate found that she was deeply befriending herself as well as her horse, and her fear abated dramatically. Yet her fear still felt like a stone, however small, hiding deep down inside. One day she found herself riding in the mythic realm, and she stepped fully into a new version of herself: "On one of our rides in the park I heard the bell ringing that I had tied to her saddle for warning hunters and bicyclists. I suddenly became Arwen, elf princess from *The Lord of the Rings*. I was riding an elfin horse who would never let me fall, and I was one with that horse. The next few times I rode, I rode again as Arwen. I am feeling healed now, no stone in my body. As we gallop up our favorite long hill, my mare and I, we are flying."

Our interconnectedness that operates at a quantum level has given birth to widespread new approaches to human suffering, to new ways of being. Eastern medicine is blending with Western medicine. Yoga and Oriental martial arts have taught Western practitioners about the energy systems of their bodies as well as their muscular power. Rather than conquest and the pursuit of excellence, people are forging more effective tools to build new paradigms of peace and partnership through such efforts as the Compassionate Listening Project, a Seattle-based nonprofit organization that teaches skills for peace building and reconciliation in families, communities, workplaces, and the world through speaking and listening from the heart during the heat of conflict.[2] Another such organization is Jean Houston's Social Artistry, which offers advanced human-development training for those working at the grassroots level in local and international community development.[3] Practitioners of energy medicine have begun to enter the field of mainstream health care alternatives, and conventional medical doctors are either incorporating these new modalities or referring patients to other practitioners. Pioneers such as Richard Gerber, MD (*Vibrational Medicine*), Michael Murphy (*The Future of the Body*), and Donna Eden (*Energy Medicine*) have written highly readable texts for popularizing these concepts.

We can explore the new frontiers of this era with our horses, whose large hearts and exquisite sensitivities call us to these new pathways. Years ago it was a horse who taught me the validity of energy work. At that time, I was somewhat skeptical about the real benefits of anything non-allopathic. I had firmly placed my belief in the conventional medical model and had not had any reason to challenge that belief. However, I did understand the principle of modern physics that we are all basically energy. That people would be justified in exploring energetic ways of healing through touch, prayer, massage, and other non-allopathic medical modes was clearly a logical extension of that fact. However, part of me wondered whether it was more a matter of the patient's belief that these things would work. This did not discount its value, but just seemed to cloud the issue and compromise the claims made.

One day my tallest lesson horse, Senior, had a new rider who had been trying to learn to ride at a trot. For a few minutes she bounced along, off and on, trying to keep her balance. When I groomed Senior the next day, he reacted violently when my brush stroked his back, to the extent that he even reached around to nip at me in his discomfort. Mostly to calm him and show him that I would not hurt him, I took my hand and made long strokes along his back on his left side, the side I could reach, but without actually touching him. My hand was just a couple of inches away from his hair. At first he backed his ears, expecting pain, but as I continued stroking, he visibly relaxed.

After several minutes, I gently touched his back with my hand, and he did not flinch. I stroked that side of his back gingerly at first, and then more confidently as I saw that he was clearly not experiencing the previous pain. Then I moved to his other side and touched it. He jumped violently away from me. To my surprise, that side was still sore. It, too, responded to my stroking just a few inches above his hair, so that in a few minutes, he was pain free on both sides of his back. As I thought about this matter, I knew that there was no mind game at work here that might have produced such results with a person. Senior was responding to my intention and the action of my hand stroking his energy field.

After that episode, I used this technique many times combined with other modalities. I became a licensed massage therapist, learning methods that benefited people as well as horses and other animals. All of these touch techniques that I learned for helping others were greatly enhanced by enlisting my imaginal body. When I stroked the energy field of a horse's swollen leg, I imagined kinesthetically that my fingers reached into the inflamed tissues and restored the energy pattern that I had picked up from the healthy leg. When I stroked a sore back, I imagined my hand reaching deeply inside the sore muscles to bring cooling relief.

Celtic lore is steeped in the intimacy of these kinds of subtle, energetic connections between people and animals. From the mythic perspective, it also wraps us in cloaks of misty landscapes and adventures with otherworldly creatures in stories such as King Arthur and Merlin; or Cerridwen, Morgan, Epona, and the druids. These stories can help us explore the inner retooling of the psyche that takes place when we undertake our hero's journey and enter the time of the belly of the whale.

Celtic heritage was pervasive throughout Europe and preceded the more familiar Greco-Roman world. Scholars such as Jean Markale make a strong case for the role of the Celts as a particularly significant and overlooked origin of our Western culture. However, historical data on the life and culture of the Celts has been inferred from the many myths that have come down to us through Christian chroniclers. These stories are populated with many animals, often fantastically configured, that, in outward form, express our inner capacities for knowing a larger version of our day-to-day world; they serve as visual expressions of the subtle, energetic world where we dwell. The very nature of the complex patterns of Celtic knots evokes a sense of how our habits are repatterned in the belly of the whale of our hero's journey. Celtic scholars speculate that many of the secrets of the Celtic ways were consciously encoded in the Celtic knots, entwining borders of art and words for preservation in the face of conquering peoples. They are like a DNA pattern for a culture, similar to how our own DNA pattern is constantly plumbed by scientists for the secrets of our own human patterns.

Celtic culture enjoys considerable popularity today. Its chthonic symbols enable us to look beyond the surface crust of our daily world. The intricate patterns of the Celts give visual form to the elements of a complex culture that has survived into today's modern world, even though the social forms have not. Their surviving Pictish art represents a spirituality anchored in the natural world, an honoring of the role of women in leadership, and a fierceness that has sustained threads of this culture in the present-day Gaelic language still spoken in parts of Ireland. Celtic knots wrap around tattooed arms and ankles. Pendants of Celtic designs adorn women's apparel. The Celts' superior skills are claimed by numerous craftsmen at Renaissance Faires and other kinds of trade shows throughout our modern world.

Epona was a feminine icon throughout the Celtic world, and her images are found throughout Britain, ancient Gaul, Yugoslavia, North Africa, and Rome. In contrast to some symbolic images of horses reflecting prestige, speed, skill in warfare, and power, Epona represents fertility and abundance, and is linked with mother-goddess forms. Many depictions show Epona as a woman bearing baskets of fruit or corn, or riding a mare sideways, or even as a mare suckling a foal. She is associated with healing waters and is considered one who accompanies the soul to the underworld, carrying a key to unlock the gates of heaven for a happy afterlife.

Morgan Llewellyn's historical novel *The Horse Goddess* gives form to her research into Celtic ways with her story of Epona. The story follows the historical blending of cultures in the eighth century BCE, reaching from the Alps across Europe to the Ukraine. In addition, it draws on the author's own experience with horses that took her to the short list of riders for the U.S. Olympic team in dressage in 1975. Just as the earlier story of Ayla demonstrated a mythic call to adventure, this story's mythic elements resonate with our own contemporary need to relate to one another with fuller awareness and sensitivity. Epona, the heroine of the story, learned her people's way of listening "hungrily for the voice of the spirit within, and was relieved each time it spoke to her, not with words but with an intuition in the blood, commands direct to the muscle and bone. She heard without ears the voice older than time."[4] She was born with a talent for subtle communication into a culture that incorporated such talent in its druidic training.

Once her village's druid priest discovered her ability to communicate with the village's ponies, he tried to force her into priestly training, taking her away from her family. In defiance of the priest, one night Epona ran away with a traveling band of men who had traded some of their own wares for her people's superior knives and ironware. Epona's intuitive ways were completely foreign to these men, and they regarded her as a liability their leader had taken on in a moment of weakness. When they encountered a group of Thracian traders along the road, a cantankerous exchange ensued, and Epona suspected that she might become an asset to be traded along with

Celtic iron swords. Instead, a loaded wagon pulled by two ponies became the object of their negotiations. As Kazhak, the leader of Epona's band, was about to close the deal, he heard Epona's urgent shout, warning him away from his negotiations because one of the horses was ill. Despite the protests of the horse's owner and the doubts of the other men, who saw only a quiet horse standing in the traces, Epona approached the mare, "its eyes red rimmed and eloquent with anguish. It suffered silently as horses must, but the pain poured from it in waves, lapping around Epona. She had to brace herself against it; she had to force herself to touch the suffering animal."[5]

When she examined the mare, she closed her eyes and "imagined something burning inside, like fire, eating the mare alive."[6] She announced to the skeptical men that the mare was poisoned and would not live long. However, as their attention turned to the mare, the men became wary, because they realized that Epona had indeed known something from far away that they had not noticed.

Then, because the men refused to help and merely watched in cynical amusement, Epona released the mare from the traces.

> Once free of the wagon, the mare reared and pawed at the sky, pulling Epona off the ground as the girl clung to her bridle. The men tried to help then, but Epona waved them back, and for some reason none of them could understand, they obeyed her. They stood in a circle, beyond the reach of the desperate, convulsing mare, and left the young woman alone with the horse.
>
> The pain was a living thing, a hand that grabbed the intestines and squeezed. The mare and Epona suffered it together, fighting with crazed fear, but fear was not sufficient. Epona tried to block off that part of her mind so she could think, concentrate. She held on grimly as the mare whirled in a circle, dragging her. She reached out with her inner being, grasping for some touch of the great fire of life, summoning its strength and support.
>
> A moment of peace came to both of them. The mare stopped her frantic struggling and stood with braced legs, fighting for breath. Epona relinquished her hold on the bridle and flattened

her body against the body of the mare, her breasts against the heaving sides, vulnerable to any move the horse might make in its dying agony. Behind her closed eyes she spoke to the spirits she knew and the unfamiliar ones that surrounded them in the place. She had not been taught the signs and invocations; she could only fashion them from her own intuitions and pray that was sufficient.

The pain had come quickly; it would kill quickly. The mare was finding it agonizing to breathe, which added to her panic. Once, her knees buckled and her forequarters sank to the ground, and Epona went down with her, holding on tightly, while the mare's driver moaned and wrung his hands. A horse down was a horse dead.

The mare's eyes were glazing, but somehow she got to her feet again, Epona clinging to her like a burr. The girl's entire being was absorbed by the pain now, but still she prayed to the spirit of life. There was nothing but the pain and the prayer.

The mare convulsed and Kazhak shouted a warning. The girl would be trampled. The mare was so wild, none of his men were willing to get close to her and pull Epona free; they could only watch helplessly as she stayed with the plunging, bellowing horses, concentrating with single-minded ferocity on the pain, pulling it, drawing it out, now . . . it will ease . . . now!

They saw her face go white beneath the golden freckles. The mare's eyes rolled in her head in the death agony, and she screamed like a human being. Her mate, still in the traces, whinnied in sympathy.

The chestnut mare stood on spraddled legs, head hanging, but she did not go down. Even as they watched, unbelieving, the glaze of death passed from her eyes. Her breathing steadied. The flow of bloody mucus from her nostrils slowed, then stopped. She raised her head and pricked her ears with interest when her teammate whinnied a second time.

Epona staggered away and flung herself down on the grass, panting.

The men crowded around her, demanding to know what she had done and how she had done it, but there was respect tinged with awe in their voices.[7]

EPONA SOON RECOVERED from her encounter with the ill mare. The experience launched her into a new phase of her life, defined by her communication with horses and her healing abilities, which brought something radically new to the world beyond her home.

The appeal of these old stories may point to an emerging validation of the trend of combining rational knowledge with intuitive understanding of bodily and environmental energies. We can learn more-organic and less-intrusive techniques to promote health in our bodies and those of our animal friends by working with touch in ways that acknowledge the energies of the body. The following activity offers you an introduction to this kind of work with a horse, but it can just as easily be used with a friend or a pet.

TRY THIS
Enhancing Your Touch

Linda Tellington-Jones developed a specialized approach to the care and training of animals, called Tellington TTouch.[8] Her method is based on circular movements of the fingers and hands all over the body. The intent of TTouch is to activate the function of the cells and awaken cellular intelligence — what she calls "turning on the electric lights of the body." TTouch fosters cooperation and respect, and offers a positive approach to training. It can improve performance and health, and presents solutions to common behavioral and physical problems in horses.

TTouch helps to release tension and increase body awareness by using a combination of specific touches, lifts, and movements. A horse responds to handling without typical fear responses. Then the horse can more easily learn new and more-appropriate behaviors. TTouch can also assist a horse with recovery from illness or injury, or simply enhance the quality of a horse's life. When you practice

TTouch, consciously using your imaginal body and listening to your physical body, the benefits of the work are greatly magnified.

GOALS

- Use your imaginal body to bring comfort to others.
- Practice sensitive touch.

PREPARATION AND EQUIPMENT

You will need one horse in an area where a horse can stand without being tied, such as a stall or small pen. Minimize distractions, such as other horses in the pen or people milling about.

Time: Forty-five minutes

Here is how to do the basic TTouch using your imaginal body to maximize the benefits. Before trying this on a horse, for example, on his shoulder, practice on your own forearm or, even better, find a friend who would enjoy a release from tight shoulders.

Imagine the face of a clock on your horse's body (or your arm or your friend's shoulder), a half inch to one inch in diameter. Place your lightly curved fingers at six o'clock on your imaginary clock, and push the skin around the face of the clock for one and a quarter circles. Place your thumb two to three inches from your forefinger and feel a connection between the thumb and forefinger. When possible, support the body gently with your free hand, placing it opposite the hand making the circle.

Whether the TTouch is light or firm, maintain a steady rhythm and constant pressure around the circle and a quarter, paying particular attention to the roundness of the circle. Be sure that your fingers do not slip on the skin as you form the circle.

Imagine that your fingers are reaching deeply and gently into the muscles of the horse and that you are waking up the cells. (When you practice this on people, they can often tell you the difference between when imaginal fingers are enlisted and when they are not.)

After each circular TTouch, you can either move to another spot at random, or you can run parallel lines on the body by making a circle, a little slide, and then another circle. Both movements induce relaxation and improve self-confidence. If you place your free hand in a supporting position and make a connection between your two hands, the horse's balance will improve and the effect of the TTouch will be enhanced.

There are times when counterclockwise circles are appropriate for releasing tension. Practice in both directions, and trust your fingers if they naturally move in a counterclockwise direction when you touch a horse.

It is helpful to learn several levels of pressure for different parts of the horse's body. To create a scale for yourself, begin with the lightest pressure by placing your thumb against your cheek. With the tip of your middle finger and the lightest possible contact, push the skin on your eyelid in a circle and a quarter. Make sure you move the skin, not just slide over it. Then repeat this movement on your forearm to practice this lightest pressure. As you do so, enlist your imaginal body for this lightest of touches. Your imaginal fingers are delicately reaching into the skin and muscles with just a whisper of a touch.

To discover and practice a firmer pressure, make several circles on your eyelid as firm as feels safe and comfortable. Repeat the circles on your forearm, noting depth and pressure. It should still be very light, and your imaginal fingers should still barely penetrate the skin.

Then, with pressure twice as deep, practice on your arm by reaching your imaginal fingers deeper into the muscle and tissue that lie beneath your fingers, allowing them to enhance pleasure and relaxation for your horse at a cellular level. This is often the pressure you would use on a person's shoulders or on much of a horse's body.

A heavier pressure also should be practiced on very muscular horses. Instead of just pressing three times deeper, tip the first joints of the fingers so that the fingernails point directly into the muscle, and apply three times the pressure. In this way, you can apply a much firmer pressure while keeping your fingers and their joints comfortable. Again, if you always approach from an intention to relax and ease the horse, your imaginal fingers will enhance the effect as they penetrate deeply into the horse's body.

Experiment with the pressure until you click into the one that feels right for the horse (or person) you are working on. Experiment with how your imaginal fingers can enhance your work. Larger or heavily muscled horses may be more responsive to the deeper pressures, but not always. If there is pain or inflammation in the body, you may have to begin the touch with a very light pressure and then establish the most effective level.

Pay attention, too, to how you stand, so that you are balanced on your two feet, and your whole body easily supports the pressure and movement of your fingers.

Experiment with aligning your breathing with that of the horse, performing one circle with your real and imaginal fingers on each out-breath.

TTouch is also very effective with pets. It can open a whole new, closer companionship with a dog or cat. With a horse, too, your attunement to the horse's physical well-being is taken to a whole new level, and training, riding, or ground work takes on a new aspect of awareness for you both.

WHEN YOU TAKE THESE SKILLS into other human interactions, you find that you have a wider palette for responding to complex situations. Coming out of the belly of the whale, where this inner work occurs, you have new tools to deal with the road of trials and adventures that awaits you farther into your hero's journey. For instance, with a horse who bucks off a rider or refuses work in other ways, Tellington TTouch advocates scanning the horse's body with sensitive fingers to find areas of tightness and discomfort. Releasing these areas with such activities as described above has shown over and over to change the behavior of the horse for work. Conflict disappears as the horse senses that his message has been heard and responded to, preventing the situation from becoming an opportunity for discipline. Similarly, in situations of human conflict, we can begin to enlist our abilities to sense the more subtle issues operating and to attend to those situations with our more highly attuned sensing, using our imaginal bodies and engaging ourselves in a new story of mythic proportions to produce a more satisfactory outcome.

CHAPTER SIX

SYMBOLS TO SUSTAIN YOU ON THE JOURNEY

Reminding Yourself of Your Deeper Path

ONCE WE DARE TO EMBARK on our hero's journey, we often need new skills to help us meet the trials and adventures confronting us along the way. In previous chapters we explored how working with horses can assist us. Inner resources such as awakened and sharpened senses, a consciously attuned imaginal body, a highly developed awareness of the power of subtle communication, and the ability to recognize opportunities for healing touch are all tools of the highly developed inner life that we can learn through the way of the horse. They offer resources for finding new approaches to daily challenges.

However, in addition to developing these inner resources, we also must attend to nurturing and sustaining them. This leads us to consider the importance of symbols in our lives. Working symbolically is often the key that makes a significant difference in any complex situation, allowing one to keep focused on the overriding higher mission or purpose.

When I worked in community development with the Institute of Cultural Affairs, training people in the necessary skills to become leaders in their local communities, one of our underlying principles was that symbols provide a major key to sustaining change.[1] When a community wished to catalyze improvement on economic, political, and cultural levels, they were encouraged to find some visible manifestation of that new direction. Although positive change was planned in all aspects of the community, something manageable and visible started the process. In one small Mexican American community in south Texas we helped a group of volunteers from the community paint their town library. Our group included a sign painter from Houston who added a large sign out front announcing the library's name and, more importantly, that improvements were afoot throughout the town. Later, several families throughout the town volunteered to paint their homes for the same purpose. Understanding the symbolic power of these actions enabled the community leaders to augment the interest generated by these relatively simple actions, engaging more citizens in the larger task at hand, which raised up local leaders who could implement the many larger projects needed to bring the poverty-ridden community a new, more prosperous future. Other communities like this one chose to anchor their plans for a new future through such activities as starting a small preschool or establishing a yearly community festival.

Horses often come into a person's life for a short-lived period to provide an important symbolic role, to lift some new understanding to consciousness through their mythic connections. One friend, Mary, relayed how horses dramatically assisted her during a difficult time in her life. As a single mother, she found herself in a relationship with a man who did not accept her young son. She allowed the man to manipulate her situation to the point that, one evening, he made it impossible for her to get to the airport on time to pick up her son, who was arriving home from a visit with his father. Instead, the couple drove down a country road far from the airport destination, leaving Mary frantic to get to the airport but helpless to contradict her lover's resistance. As he drove she noticed a herd of horses galloping in the field next to their car.

With a sudden impulse, she insisted that he stop the car. As she approached the fence, a dozen of the horses swerved and galloped over to her, blowing noisily over the fence. She was overwhelmed with the power and vitality that emanated from them, their breath pulsing all around her. She vividly remembered the hours she had spent on horseback as a child on her family farm, riding to do daily chores. For the first time she recognized the intimacy and support those horses from the past had given her, and now, many years later, she was ready and able to take in the energy of this strange band of wild horses. It was as though their breath were infusing her with their power and restoring her own power in the process. She stepped back into the car with a new, clear determination for what was right in her life, aware that the horses had symbolically brought her back to her own center. She knew that this was the last time she would be victimized by this man.

Children in crisis are sometimes fortunate to have a horse come into their lives as a symbol of a pathway to a more positive future. At the age of nine, Andy was the oldest of three children, and his story typifies those encountered in therapeutic riding programs that have a mental health component. Andy's single mother was illiterate and struggled to support her three children by cleaning houses. Andy's alcoholic father had traumatized his younger life before leaving the family two years previously. In school, Andy did not have close friends and readily fought with others. He had difficulty with his schoolwork. He was at a critical time in his young life when he might soon be headed for more serious trouble. When more traditional efforts to help Andy did not work, his teachers suggested that he might benefit from the local therapeutic riding program. There, a team consisting of a therapeutic riding instructor, a psychotherapist, and a case manager worked with Andy to create a plan to give him better skills with his peers and with himself. He was paired with a small horse who had recently joined the program and had experienced similar early years of abuse. Clearly expecting something unpleasant, the horse turned away when Andy approached, avoiding his touch. As Andy learned how to earn the horse's trust, he taught himself how to trust.

The techniques his instructor taught him for his horse were soon taught to Andy's mother as effective communication tools for her to incorporate into her family's life. She learned how to encourage Andy's new skills at home and to more effectively interact with her other children. Before long, Andy prided himself on his ability to lead the horse through a complicated obstacle course that he had completely refused to approach weeks before. He could ask the horse to carry items on his back that previously the horse would not have allowed Andy even to bring near him. At home, his mother began to experience a new spirit of cooperation in her household and was able to find the time to enroll in a literacy course. By exploring the symbolic aspect of this little horse's presence, positive change began in a way that had not succeeded with other, previously attempted interventions.

In our own lives, we can harness the power of symbols for our personal purposes. In fact, the power of symbols operates in our lives whether we are conscious of it or not. It is often interesting to point out to teenagers that the chaotic state of their bedrooms is symbolic of other areas of their lives. Further, if they change even a small corner of their room from its characteristic chaos to a small patch of order and intentionality, and attend to it daily with even just a glance, beneficial change will result in other aspects of their lives. Feng shui, the Chinese art of harmoniously positioning objects in buildings and other places, is based on the principle of harnessing the power of the elements in your surroundings to catalyze and support positive change in your life.

Bringing the power of symbol into one's life is an important tool for negotiating the trials and adventures of the mythic life. All the world's religions understand this, with their icons and other symbols, including rituals, to remind and inspire followers and sustain them as they live and work in the world. Our increasingly secular world is poorer for having lost a connection with these ancient rituals and symbols without replacing them with something equally meaning-ful. People become influenced by symbols that cannot anchor them in their own deeper stories, such as the trademarks of Coca-Cola, Star-bucks, Toyota, and all the other symbols of a materialistic orienta-tion. Inner whisperings often emerge of a life not fully lived, not fully understood, not deeply and passionately embraced. Carl Jung ob-served in *Man and His Symbols*: "It is the role of religious symbols to give a meaning to the life of man. . . . Modern man does not under-stand how much his 'rationalism' (which has destroyed his capacity to respond to numinous symbols and ideas) has put him at the mercy of the psychic 'underworld'. . . . We have stripped things of their mystery and numinosity; nothing is holy any longer."[2]

Alongside the commercial symbols of our modern world is the symbolic power of our beautiful blue planet viewed from space, of-fering us an inspiring vision of our planet as one world, instead of a collection of separate countries with competing or warring factions. This vision reminds us of the possibility for making that oneness more manifest in our daily lives. Recent generations are the first to have grown up with that symbol as part of their everyday lives. As with understanding ourselves as energetic beings, understanding our planet as one global community requires a radical restructuring of our thinking. It requires that we draw on new capacities to cope with the complexity and challenges that this restructuring entails. We must step into the future before us, anchored in our vision of a possible bright future for ourselves and the world.

We have important choices along these lines, because another symbol that looms for us is the image of the atomic bomb that exploded in Hiroshima — a symbol of our capacity to actually destroy our planet. Our choices lie in how we respond to that possibility. Images of our future world held in our minds and allowed to inspire our daily actions become powerful symbols that guide how we create the future. Simply protesting war has never eliminated it. "Stop War" is essentially holding in our minds the image of war, regardless of our passionate protests. Instead, we must turn our attention to actions, words, and symbols of a viable alternative to war, and make this focus powerful enough to compete in boardrooms and political meeting places to effectively tackle the animosities that lead to destructive conflict.

One small way that this is beginning to happen is that, in many communities, a flag of planet Earth flies alongside that of our country. One gift that horses bring us is the opportunity to learn new ways of being on this beautiful planet. This reaches way beyond the obvious connection they provide for maintaining our connection with the natural world, one so easily eclipsed with the demands of modern life. By becoming partners and teachers of a new way of being, horses also offer us ways to empower ourselves for making a positive difference in our world. Once we acknowledge the power that horses can bring into our lives, we need to claim symbols that root that power deeply within us so that we can carry it over the long haul through our everyday lives. We need potent reminders.

One easy way to do that is to nail a horseshoe over your door. Ancient peoples did that. Some said that the upturned ends symbolized holding good luck. Its shape for this purpose evokes the crescent moon, a symbol for Isis and other moon-related goddesses, so that the horseshoe as moon-crescent becomes a talisman for protection. As Gerald and Loretta Hausman explain in *The Mythology of Horses*, "Once hung upward above the door, it asked for the benevolent spirit of the Great Mother to guard all the people inside of the house. And the winged foot of the horse carried this prayer straight to the moon herself."[3]

Others say the downturned ends symbolize an open portal or door-way, and indicate welcome. Still others have tied this configuration to the last letter of the Greek alphabet, the omega symbol, which it re-sembles. Perhaps for early Christians it was a reminder of beliefs taught by people like Clement of Alexandria, who spoke of the word of God as "the Alpha and the Omega of Whom alone the end becomes begin-ning, and ends again at the original beginning without any break."[4]

IN RECENT DECADES Native American spirituality has emerged into the awareness of the rest of the world with abundant stories and be-liefs that rely on a rich symbolic life, bringing us closer to our natu-ral world. In the sun dance, for example, the rhythms of the drums, the days-long dancing around a sacred tree, and the chanting call to-gether the community for spiritual sustenance for the coming year. These events are enriched with potent fetishes, medicinal plants, and the elements of nature's forces. Loretta Afraid of Bear Cook relates how horses have functioned symbolically for her entire community, the Oglala Sioux, at the annual Afraid of Bear American Horse Sun Dance, located at the Wild Horse Sanctuary near Hot Springs, South Dakota.[5] Since 1994 her people, and others who have joined with them, have spent four days gathered during the summer solstice for the tribe's most important spiritual event.

During the four days of nonstop dancing, when several men and women dance on behalf of their whole community, the large wild-mustang herd, protected in a sanctuary by the land's owner, has a special role. The horses encircle the group and stay for the duration of the dance, protecting them from snakes and any other threats to their safety. Being wild horses with little or no human interaction, they keep their distance, but those who choose to stay around the group of men and women appear to take a protective stance. Though their many hoofprints show that they normally spend time in the arbor, where the dance takes place, they keep a respectful distance during the dancing. They quietly surround the arbor for the night, and leave during each day, returning each night again to take their protective stance. All of the people are aware of the horses' presence and appreciate the way the horses honor the humans' presence. The prayers that the dancers receive from the spirit realm through their dance always include at least one message of protection for the horses. The horses have become important participants in the sun dance.

Although horses entered Native American culture relatively recently, having been brought by conquering Spaniards in the seventeenth century, horses readily became an important part of the Native American world. A Navajo war song includes the horse in their landscape. The horse's anatomy provides symbolic reference points for larger realities, and anchors the horse's mythic role for the warrior:

> My horse has a hoof like striped agate.
> His fetlock is like a fine eagle plume.
> His legs are like quick lightning.
> My horse's body is like an eagle-plumed arrow.
> My horse has a tail like a trailing black cloud.
> His mane is made of short rainbows.
> My horse's ears are made of round corn.
> My horse's eyes are made of big stars.
> My horse's head is made of mixed waters
> From the holy springs, he never knows thirst.
> My horse's teeth are made of white shell.
> The long rainbow is in his mouth for a bridle,
> And with it I guide him.[6]

This song seeds our imagination, accompanying more-common knowledge of the horse's parts so that they become symbols of physical power, graceful movement, sensitivity, heart centeredness, the great outdoors, and other important aspects of the horse's place in our lives.

AS DO MANY OTHER TRADITIONS, Native Americans use the mandala as a symbolic tool, in the form of sand paintings and the medicine wheel. A mandala reflects the circular nature of life. Once we look, this circle appears everywhere: in such things as sliced tomatoes, blossoming flowers, spiral galaxies, spiderwebs, tree-trunk rings, and nautilus shells. Creating a mandala in the form of a sand painting or a medicine wheel is an exercise in orienting oneself within larger patterns of life.

Judith Cornell's pioneering work with creating mandalas has revealed this tool's extraordinary potential for healing. When struggling with cancer, she created mandalas and experienced a spiritual awakening. The creative process enabled her to find a healing power within herself and to recover from a sense of psychological fragmentation brought by a clash between the scientific worldview and her intuitive experiences of wholeness and luminous states of consciousness. Since that time, she has led thousands of people into their innate gifts of creativity, spirituality, and wholeness through her writings and programs that synthesize art with psychology, philosophy, science, and spirituality.[7]

The Native American medicine wheel places us within six directions, creating a three-dimensional mandala: north, south, east, west, sky above, and earth below. Invoking the directions at the beginning of any event, even at the start of the day, encourages us to remain grounded in the natural world around us, enabling us to understand our daily tasks within a larger framework for our lives. There are various qualities, animals, and colors associated with the medicine wheel, and it contains either four or six poles. One version is expressed in the following way:

> East — The place of the dawn and new beginnings, as each day provides us an open possibility for starting anew. Its color is yellow or gold and is associated with springtime, air, and the eagle.
>
> South — The place of passion that fuels our lives, giving us inspiration and energy for our work in the world. Its

color is red and is associated with summertime, fire, and
the wolf.

West — The place of the sunset and completion or introspection, going into shadows and darkness. Its color is
black and is associated with autumn, water, and the bear.

North — The place of wisdom, where lessons from the past
are incubated and assimilated. Its color is white and is associated with winter, earth, and the buffalo.

Above — The place of spirit and our ancestors who accompany us. It is associated with the sky, fathering, and birds.

Below — The place of our daily tasks, living within nature
as we complete the cycle of our lives within the medicine
wheel. It is associated with the earth, mothering, and
the dog.

According to the Native American tradition, each person is born
into a particular beginning place on the wheel, and that place defines
the easy way throughout that person's life. However, to live only in
one part of the medicine wheel means to be only a partial person.
For instance, people who possess the wisdom of the north may be
cold and unfeeling if they do not incorporate the passion from the
south, introspection from the west, fresh approaches from the east,
the ancestors' presence from above, and the richness of the earth from
below. Only by traveling to the other parts of the wheel in one's lifetime can a person become a whole being.

Hyemeyohsts Storm's delightful story of Jumping Mouse is a
parable based on this understanding of the medicine wheel and also
a tale of a tiny hero's journey. Mouse hears a call to adventure in the
form of the rushing water of a nearby river that none of the other
mice can hear. Despite the ridicule of his fellow mice, he eventually
sets out for the sacred mountain that he had glimpsed from the side
of the river where he was named Jumping Mouse. Along the way, he

courageously encounters several trials and adventures, and receives help from allies Frog, Old Mouse, Buffalo, and Wolf, who represent various directions on the wheel of Jumping Mouse's life. However, because he offered his eyes in exchange for their help, he finally approaches the sacred mountain blind and mortally fearful of his worst enemy, Eagle. In the end, he falls asleep as an eagle swoops down upon him. On awakening, he is astonished to find that he is alive and able to see again. He has become Eagle, and as Frog encourages him to jump high and trust the wind, he finds himself flying and able to see all the earth below from a higher vantage point than he had ever seen previously as a tiny mouse.[8]

This little story gives substance and narrative to the symbol of the medicine wheel, often represented as a circle divided into four quadrants and filled with each of the colors of the four directions. It visually reminds us that we all have the opportunity to live our own version of this tale, to travel all the directions of the wheel in our lives toward becoming a full person.

Tibetan Buddhist traditions incorporate sand-mandala creation in the Kalachakra initiation. They create mandalas as tools for reconsecrating the earth and its inhabitants. When a mandala is finished after many days of work by teams of monks, the colored sands are swept up and usually poured into a nearby river, where the waters carry the energy of the consecration out into the world. It is inspiring and meditative to participate in this mandala creation as the watcher, while a group of monks works with diligence, artistry, and sacred intention over many hours and days. Something changes in the atmosphere, and a tangible experience of peace is created for all people who participate. Later in this chapter you will have an opportunity to create a mandala of your own for anchoring the symbolic power of the horse in your own life.

Another meditation involving a mandala form is walking a

labyrinth, a circular maze that leads one into a center point and then back out again. One has the opportunity to engage the whole body, not just the mind, in a meditation. Walking into the middle, you mentally focus on an issue that you wish to leave behind. The intent is that, upon arrival in the middle of the labyrinth, you reach a center point between the past and future. When you feel ready, you begin the walk outward, back along the same path but in reverse, claiming some new possibility for that issue or leaving behind the old to embrace the new.

Several forms of labyrinths have become popular in the past twenty years, derived from Native American cultures and pre-Christian cultures in Europe. The most complex of these is the eleven-circuit pattern from the floor of Chartres Cathedral in France. A person walks into the pattern starting at the outer edge, and eventually arrives in the middle with several 180-degree twists and turns at each quadrant of the circle. A feeling of neural integration occurs, with the whole being brought into balance by walking the pattern. In this way, with four distinct quadrants that are similar to our brain's division into four quadrants, the walking of the labyrinth simultaneously balances the mind and body. Due to the international work of Lauren Artress and the Labyrinth Project from Grace Cathedral in San Francisco, there are literally thousands of labyrinths like this all over the world now.

Linda Tellington-Jones pioneered work with labyrinths and horses many years ago, teaching young horses to better balance their bodies, to increase awareness of foot placement, and to go beyond instinctive behavior. Labyrinth work encourages a horse to focus his attention on the human handler and on his own body. These labyrinths usually involve a simple form with three or four turns, laid out in an arena with PVC pipe or jump poles on the ground.

June Gunter and Beth Hyjek have constructed a simple labyrinth of another kind at their ranch for their TeachingHorse programs in Rogue River, Oregon.[9] It is based on the Cretan labyrinth form, which is simpler than the Chartres Cathedral labyrinth, and is large enough for a person to ride or walk through the pattern with a horse. June and Beth have found that giving others the opportunity to walk the labyrinth with horses has deepened participants' understanding of the subtle and interactive ways that horses partner with people. They ask participants in their workshops to view the walk into the labyrinth as a journey to the center and back, a typical use of the labyrinth with the added dynamic of remaining grounded and in partnership along the way. They ask them to notice what comes to their attention on the way and what the horse teaches them. Powerful insights come from allowing the symbolic meaning of the experience to be felt in the body. "Getting the mental insight into your body is the gift here," says June.

One woman, for instance, entered this Oregon labyrinth needing more energy for an important project. She held her shoulders tight and high. Although the horse started at her side, he began giving her little nudges along the way, as if to say, "Let's get going on this!" until they arrived in the middle. There, she made a conscious effort to release her resistance to the project. Her shoulders dropped, and her breathing deepened. Others watching noticed that the horse dropped his head and breathed deeply as well. After a few minutes she began walking out again, clearly more energized. The horse moved along with her, without nudging at all until they were near the end of the labyrinth, when he nudged her once again. She reported that, to her amazement, the nudge had come exactly when she momentarily had thought of what she was leaving behind, peeking for a moment at her previous resistance. Although those watching saw no noticeable outward change in her demeanor, the horse seemingly had picked up on the change in her thinking and had encouraged her as he best knew how.

As another woman and her horse walked through the labyrinth, the horse suddenly turned around and went the other direction, stepping out of the labyrinth pattern. When she reflected on what had happened, this woman saw an important metaphor emerging. Her pattern was to begin projects and then, in the middle, revert to old habits. The horse's behavior gave her a chance to see that pattern and think about how to respond in a new way. She could get frustrated, which was her usual response to herself. Or she could gently take the horse back on track and simply get going again, without anger and recrimination. That way worked much better for the horse, and she realized it was a better choice for herself as well. Sometimes she reflected that it might even be good for the horse and her to return to the center and start over again. The gift in this process was that she experienced this insight in a physical context, moving it out of her mind and into action with her body. This gave her whole being an opportunity to learn a new pattern, something not readily possible through merely discussing and mentally understanding the issue.

Negotiating the sharp turns in the labyrinth often is a disorganized experience, simply because people do not plan ahead for how to best negotiate the turns. This becomes an opportunity to practice looking farther ahead to prepare, instead of reacting in the immediate moment. The horse then feels a sense of being prepared for success instead of needing correction in the moment. The metaphor offers a wonderful reorientation for how to be in relationships of all kinds, planning ahead for unexpected twists and turns. With the labyrinth walk providing a symbolic framework, the dance of relationship becomes more beautiful.

WHEN WE RECOGNIZE AND WORK WITH POTENT SYMBOLS in our lives, we can observe how animals intersect with our story symbolically to provide information and wisdom. Animals often appear symbolically in one's life to give support at a time when a deeper story is coming through. In this case, the animal often appears in dream form or some other metaphorical manner. My friend, Skye Burn, was turning away from a career in the corporate world and discovering her new work in aligning leadership and creativity. Her father had long ago engendered in her a respect for the eagle as a bird of high purpose and extraordinary beauty. She sometimes wished she had an eagle of her own to empower her in this new journey. One day she was out hiking and came upon the body of an eagle in full feathers lying in her path. The bird had recently died and had not yet been ravaged by vultures. She was astonished and empowered with this gift for which she had yearned. It allowed her to renew herself with the high purpose that the eagle signified to her and to engage afresh the challenges that her new career presented.

Artist Denise Kester bases her extraordinarily imaginative and original art on her intimate connection with animals who appear in her dreams and in her life. Crows are a primary symbol for her and are the main image in the logo for her company, Drawing on the Dream. She studies their many appearances in the trees surrounding her home, as well as in her dreams, where they evoke a language of the soul that she expresses in her art with images and poetry. Recently, for the first time in her life, a blue horse began to appear in her dreams over several months' time. She had vaguely noticed a blue horse in the first dream, in which she had been given three important guiding phrases: "Stay in your heart. Remember who you really are. Trust your instincts." In a second dream, she restlessly awoke preoccupied with intense remorse over a dream horse that she had neglected for a long time: "I have forgotten and neglected the horse, my horse. I am on my way to feed him. He is surrounded by fire and smoke. I am concerned that he is frightened by the smells and noise. He is trapped in his stall, waiting, not patiently. I have brought food. I feel ashamed at myself for forgetting that I had a horse. I am reluctant to face him because of my dereliction. I am worried about the condition I will find him [in]."[10]

Tossing and turning, she fell asleep again and dreamed of little fuzzy horses sitting in a tree with several crows. The image of horses sitting side by side with her most potent animal ally got her attention in a fresh way. She began to earnestly try to hear the message that the horse offered her.

I woke up and read about [the] horse, symbolically and historically. I was born in the Chinese year of the horse. [The] horse represents some of these things: horsepower, movement, transition, transportation through difficult times, freedom, and the power that comes with being free. I read that a horse is a teacher standing grounded and yet not constrained by earth. They can fly like the wind.

I know that I am longing for freedom from decisions and responsibility. Can [the] horse take me into this new, uncharted territory? For the first time in my life, I don't know what I want, [and I'm] wondering if here is where I want to be. I am a teacher, artist, businesswoman, wife, mother, homeowner and gardener, visionary, responsible citizen. How can [the] horse help me?[11]

She began to realize that the blue horse was connected to the fact that she wrestled with major transitions in her life: she had started a new career as a teacher of weekend workshops, and her way of actually doing art was dramatically shifting. Instead of just teaching technique, which she had done for years, she addressed the deeper issues surrounding the creative process, such as fear and understanding one's own vision. For the first time she trusted her deeper instincts about life and the creative process and had started to teach others how to tap into their own creativity, to stand in front of a group of people and talk about her personal process.

In the next dream, in the distance she saw a dark horse hitched to a buggy coming toward her. When he finally came closer, she noticed: "He is not black, as I thought he was at a distance. He is a deep midnight blue. He is huge. He is free from the buggy. He does have a bridle with thick, strong leather reins that are hung over his neck. He is looking at me shyly, yet intently. I have the feeling that he wants me to come to him as he has come to me. Maybe I can help him find his home."[12]

A shy and quiet person at heart, Denise felt that she had been asked by the blue horse to get up on its back and ride into her new future, however fearful she might feel. For her it was bound with profound issues of partnership, entering a new life after age fifty, more freely expressing her inner thinking, and trusting the process of exposing herself with others. It was time to get on the horse and ride, time to step into a new and more powerful role for others, with increased visibility in teaching art as a way of knowing life and as a spiritual path. The blue horse became a powerful symbol of an inner part of herself that beckoned her onward. She continued relaying the dream:

> I approach him slowly so as not to startle him. I have to stand on my tiptoes to reach the bit at his mouth, to gently pull his head down so that I can reach the reins. I lead him by the reins from my yard. He follows me easily. He is graceful, gentle, and magnificent. We are walking on the grass in the opposite direction [to] that he has come from. This seems odd to me because if I want to find whom he belongs to, then I should head in the direction that he has come from, but no part of him or me wants to go that way. The horse seems relieved and content, and so am I. The ground is easy to walk on. The grass is green and the terrain is gently rolling. I can see mountains in the distance. The sun is warm. I see a large oak tree that is partially fallen over. While holding onto the reins I climb up onto the tree so that I can try to get onto the horse. I do this and find that it is easier than I thought it would be. I have a curious sensation when I am on the back of the horse. It is as if I fit him like a glove. This feels like the most right thing I've done in a long time. Even though there is no saddle I feel secure and safe. I am a part of him, and he is a part of me. I don't know what we will find, but with him I do feel a sense of direction and momentum. I know now that this is my horse. Together we are home. I can see clearly and further into the distance. I have no fear.[13]

To help her explore and remember the blue horse's message, Denise incorporates its image into her art, holding before her, as a reminder, the symbol of riding powerfully into her new life.

FOR MYSELF, THE HORSE IS A LONGTIME ALLY, having shown up early to become a lifelong companion. However, at a time of major change several years ago, the turtle came to me in symbolic form. My family and I had contemplated a move from San Antonio, where we had lived for nearly twenty years. At one point, I felt overwhelmed with the complexity of the enterprise: To where exactly should we move? How could we adequately involve everyone in the family in the decision? How would we deal with such necessary tasks as selling our home, parting with old friends, arranging for the sale of some horses, and shipping others with us? There seemed to be one big decision after another. I yearned for a deeper guidance for negotiating this journey.

One night I spent hours lying awake and asked for a dream that would assist me. Finally I drifted off to sleep and dreamed briefly of a huge turtle that was munching away at grass and was so fat that it seemed about to burst from its shell. It pushed its way just beneath the grassy sod that moved up over its back like an earthy blanket, taking mouthfuls of grass as it moved along its way. Although I clearly remembered this image when I awoke, I had no idea of its significance and actually felt a bit disappointed. Beyond an occasional box turtle that we'd found as children and kept for a few days before releasing, I'd not paid much attention to turtles.

Later that day, however, I flew to visit my mother for the first time in two years. My brother picked me up at the airport and said we first had to stop at the pet store for food for his pet snapping turtle, which in just one year had grown to become huge. I was astonished at this mention of a live, oversized turtle so soon after the previous night's dream. Later, when I walked into my mother's home, the one new piece in her living room was a golden, life-sized turtle sculpture on a living room table. That was enough. I settled into studying what the turtle represented for other cultures, as a way to understand its appearance in my life at this time.

I found that Native American cultures understand the earth as a giant turtle island on which we all live. In Chinese medicine the turtle represents the element of water and moisture, one of the five elements: earth, air, fire, wood, metal, and water. In other cultures, the turtle represents the quality of patiently traveling the path to finish ahead of the wild hare. A Japanese tale tells of a boy who travels to the bottom of the sea on the back of a turtle. He spends time in that kingdom for many years, finally returning home with a box that, when opened, turns him into an old man. Turtle thus reveals his talent for longevity. There is a tribal community in the African country of Senegal that reveres turtles as bearers of divine messages to and from mankind. Turtles travel close to the earth, responding in a reptilian manner to its rhythms, carrying their own protection by simply withdrawing into their shell.

I considered all these stories of the turtle as they related to me. I remembered that, a few years previously, I had taken several days for personal reflection at a silent retreat. Sitting on my shelf now was a real turtle shell that had attracted my attention at the beach, when those gathered at Lebh Shomea had been allowed to speak freely to one another for one day a week. One of the nuns had insisted that I take it home with me. Looking back, I realized that the silence of that time began my turn to focus serious attention on my spiritual life. The turtle shell had appeared when I had begun to slow down my life before I, too, became an empty shell. In the context of our family's move, I began to understand that the turtle had shown up when I needed to slow down and take things one step at a time, staying grounded to what I knew was important instead of charging ahead with the myriad of details that called for attention. Sure enough, as I took this advice into myself, evoked by the turtle's presence, everything began to easily work its way out. The most difficult decisions became easier. On the day before we put it on the market, our house suddenly had the perfect buyer. Everything seemed to flow with an ease that previously had been out of reach.

Recently, as I began a three-week trip to Turkey, a trip that factored in finalizing this book, the turtle showed up again. I accidentally printed out a photograph of a turtle from my computer instead of a photo of my granddaughter that I had planned to take with me. Amused at the mistake, I tucked the turtle photo in with the others. A few hours later my daughter called to tell me that she and my granddaughter had spent the morning playing with turtles in a nearby stream. As I packed my bags for the trip, I found a little notebook I had tucked into my suitcase weeks earlier, one that had lain around for years, and with a start, I noticed that it held a simple drawing of a turtle on its cover, resembling a mandala.

With all that, having had no visitation from the turtle for over fourteen years, I became watchful on my travels. Sure enough, after about a week, I walked down ancient stairs into the oracle site of the Apollo center at Didyma, the only time I was in front of the group, and was greeted by a large, live tortoise, measuring about sixteen inches across, at the foot of the stairs. He was remarkably curious, and moved among our group, eagerly looking around at us, and was joined by two other tortoises a bit later. The next two days, we saw turtles each day, and then no more. But I had gotten the message by then. The turtles had all shown up at oracle sites, places where ancient peoples had gone for messages from another dimension, from a divine, higher source. Like the Senegalese, who revered turtles for their oracular talents, I seemed to be surrounded by turtles who asked me to pay attention to that aspect of my own life. I noticed that the numerous mosques dotting the Turkish landscape resembled turtles; they seemed to be a kind of holy version of the turtle. In fact, at one point, as we lay beneath the dome of the fourteenth-century Turkish bath, or hammam, in Istanbul, a friend pointed out that the experience seemed like lying inside of a turtle and looking up through the star-shaped openings of its shell to the blue sky above.

For me, the concrete message from the turtle was to ground my writing in its higher purpose. The essential work of *Riding into Your*

Mythic Life is to encourage a radical, fundamental reorientation of ourselves to the world around us. Work with horses accomplishes this by giving us experiences that connect us with our highest selves. It energizes us for pursuing our greatest dreams and hopes. We come to treat everything as sentient. We participate in growing a membrane that is a kind of web embracing the earth, increasing in density and activating new consciousness. We understand how things fit together in one great story, a story of evolution of a new era. We join with other great specialists of spirit who are leading people into their full potential. We become pilgrims of the future, each here to bring some dream into reality by living our own journey to the fullest. The turtle tells me to remember to slow down and engage this deeper purpose of my partnership with horses.

WHEN ENGAGED IN THE TRIALS AND ADVENTURES of our hero's journey, we need powerful symbolic tools to sustain our vision and remind us of the larger path that we tread. The demands of modern life make these symbolic underpinnings a necessity. In the face of hectic lifestyles, a kind of amnesia often takes hold. It can happen in the face of entropy setting in, when the lure of the interminable lazy afternoons becomes distractingly soporific. We lose our inspiration and enthusiasm for the journey. Or, in the stress of a particularly demanding time, it is easy to forget what we know about taking care of ourselves. Distraction and discouragement are often the stuff of classical heroes' adventures. Ulysses spent years on Calypso's island with extraordinary foods and a beautiful nymph. His men ate lotuses and no longer wanted to bother with the journey home. Bilbo Baggins was tempted to snatch back the ring of power from Frodo.

Today, upwardly mobile Westerners sometimes experience a sense of self-betrayal by their affluent lifestyles. They leave their homes early to return late after a long daily commute, their communities resembling ghost towns during the day. These men and women lock themselves into jobs that pay their ever-escalating expenses but ignore the niggling desire to engage in the deeper journey that calls them. As a result, they often develop serious health problems. Yet, affluence continues to have a hold on their imaginations, fed by the media's encouragement of the acquisitive lifestyle. Stepping into any other lifestyle feels like failure by the standards of our culture. People feel caught between the promise of happiness in buying more, and the fear of failure, a place where a sense of desperation quietly tightens its firm grip on their health and their lives. They know that something is wrong but they do not know what to do about it. Knowing that they were called to some adventure long ago and lost their way, they are stuck in the cultural trance of our times. The road of trials can challenge a person this way. One may have set forth with high intentions for life, only to find that the way has been lost. The following activity can help you remember your way and stay on track.

TRY THIS
Your Shield of Power

To remind yourself of the path of your own journey, you can make a personal shield to assist you, a mandala that reminds you of your place in your larger life, anchored in the heart and power of the horse at its center. For this shield of power, you will want to explore your animal allies in addition to the horse. Try not to choose an animal that appeals to you for its beauty or power. Rather, take the receptive attitude of asking what animal chooses you, so that it can share its particular skills and wisdom. Each animal holds a particular embodiment of spirit, a particular special strength and skill.

From the Native American perspective, Jamie Sams and David Carson's *Medicine Cards* provide a rich resource for becoming acquainted with this special way of understanding our interactions with the natural world around us. If you are not already aware of a particular animal having chosen to accompany you recently, it is often quite enlightening simply to mindfully request wisdom concerning an important issue in your life while drawing a medicine card from the deck. What animal is pictured on the card that you drew? See if the writings about that animal offer something helpful to you. For the purposes of this activity, you can accept that animal as your ally.

A simpler way to discover your animal ally is to take a short walk outside, holding your intention to find an animal for this activity, and notice what animal first claims your attention, be it an ant, bird, dog, cat, or whatever. Trust that it has come to you for a valid purpose at this particular time, and spend some time reflecting on the symbolic meaning of this animal for your life situation.

This activity is not about being an artist or creating something beautiful. It is about creating powerful symbols for sustaining yourself. It is often challenging to trust our own creative abilities for such an intuitive experience. Take a deep breath and promise yourself that you will trust that whatever is created is good. Ask your inner critic to step outside the door for now, or tell her that you will honor her opinions and incorporate them as best you can.

GOALS

- Create a personal mandala to remind you of your own hero's journey.
- Explore symbols that can meaningfully support your journey.
- Empower yourself to make new choices for day-to-day life.

PREPARATION AND EQUIPMENT

- Paper plate or other circular form
- Markers for coloring
- Glue stick

- Horse magazines, and other magazines and image sources
- Scissors

Time: One hour

Draw lines to divide the circle of your paper plate into four quadrants. In the center of the mandala you will glue a picture of a horse, cut from a magazine or drawn by you, symbolizing your partnership with a beautiful, powerful, and heart-centered sentient being. The paper plate will be your shield.

Take a few minutes to write a praise song to the horse for what it means in your life, and write those words on the back of your shield.

In each of the four quadrants, draw or find images that represent the following for you personally:

1. Your Strengths and Talents — What do you know that you carry with you in life; for example, such qualities as loyalty, friendship, or endurance? Is it a talent for a particular sport? (Teens often find it helpful to ask a friend to help with this one.) By now, if you've worked with a horse in the experiences outlined previously, you have glimpsed some of your more subtle abilities. One of the gifts of a therapeutic riding environment is that people with disabilities help us all to see that we have our own gifts and challenges. We all struggle with the warts of being human. As a friend of mine says, "A normal person is just someone you don't know very well." And if you are having a bad day and can't think of a single thing that you'd consider to be a strength, then take a walk or call a friend, and notice that you are able to do those things. Start with those strengths and list others as they come to mind.

2. Your Fears — It is in facing and conquering your fears that some of your most potent power is released. Have

these fears clearly in mind, even if you haven't figured out how to deal with them yet. They will become some of your most powerful teachers as you get more acquainted with them.

3. Your Hopes and Dreams — Give them some juicy colors and be bold in what you seek. Include material things, such as a car or a home, along with more intangible desires, such as relationships you wish to build and such broader dreams as world peace or creating homes for all the world's children. You can cut out items from magazines representing your hopes and dreams.

4. Your Animal Allies — Who are the animals asking to accompany you on the journey? Who has been there with you in the past? Find a photo or make a drawing of these companions that you can surround with colors and shapes that appeal to you.

Spend some time filling in all the white space with color or designs so that the shield becomes substantial in its visual impact.

Then, place this shield by the door of your bedroom or your front door so that you pass by it each day. As you pass through that doorway, however briefly, you make a pledge to carry those qualities and commitments into your day. The shield reminds you of the story of your life. It will protect and guide you.

AS YOU TRAVEL THROUGH FURTHER ADVENTURES, you will find that claiming items for symbolic significance will sustain the power of those events. These items keep you connected with the imaginal realm where your mythic life unfolds its rich story. You may carry a special rock in your pocket to remind you of some gift. You might create a bracelet of beads signifying the transcendent importance of each hour of your day. In fact, the more you give symbolic form to your experience in any way you choose, whether through art, movement, or storytelling, you further the unfolding of your own story at the mythic level of the self. You give your story form, strength, and a life of its own, populated by more than the humdrum flesh and blood of daily existence. Your story has a higher reference in an imaginal world that relies primarily on your creation, informing and strengthening your path in the day-to-day world.

CHAPTER SEVEN

YOUR LIFE AS SACRED THEATER

Claiming Treasures through Ritual

NOWHERE IS THE MYTHIC ASPECT OF OUR LIVES more apparent than in such highly dramatic times as when some long-desired goal is attained. We feel a tangible experience of the brushstrokes that make our lives unique and vibrant. After hard effort, we've at last arrived at the mountaintop. Maybe we've found a wildly improbable and perfect love of our life. Perhaps some wonderful and unexpected gift has come our way: we have received an unexpected, huge insurance settlement or an inheritance, or an anonymous friend has left thousands of dollars in an unmarked envelope on our front porch just when we needed it (which actually happened to me). Maybe we have finally found some redeeming truth in a situation of great suffering. Everything now becomes illuminated by a glow with our ordinary experience taking on new vitality. We are riding high on life.

When we have just gained a boon, we can gaze back at what led us to this point and experience a new perspective on it. We notice the patterns that guided us to our accomplishment. For the first time (or once again but from a fresh perspective) we see how our personal story shares common elements with the best movies, stories, and theater we have known. We have a sense that our own life is storied and that the seemingly random events of our past are newly organized into a meaningful pattern for us, enhancing the power of the moment.

In our partnership with horses in past times, the boon may have been blue ribbons at advancing levels of horse shows, culminating in national or even international competition. At their best, horse shows offer us opportunities to work toward our personal-performance best and to bring our horses to their personal best. When we have worked for months and years toward this end, the process becomes a hero's journey, and we gain the boon of recognition before a crowd of appreciative fans.

A natural outgrowth of our work with horses on the farm or in sports, this kind of competition has been replaced by something new. Most of us come to horses from busy modern lives that are framed by concrete pathways to office buildings and meetings, long commutes, quests for quality family time, and attempts to survive complex lives. Horses now lead us to a boon of a different sort. They bring us to the hidden treasures within ourselves, the treasures that reveal themselves in partnership, through our exploring the ability to communicate with and honor other sentient beings. These treasures are a compassionate heart and a mind that is open to previously untapped capacities for the large endeavors required for our world, capacities we find when listening to the whispers and intuitions of our more fully developed selves. And too, we find that we are in love with our world, not because it is broken, but because it calls to our hearts and it is sacred. We are anchored in joy as the underlying principle of life, which may not look like happiness but is rich, full, and beautiful anyway. The compassionate heart joins with a mind that hears and understands the power of our body's subtle intuitions to enlist critical and powerful tools for building a new world. From this heart and mind we can forge new pathways for ourselves and others, build bridges between cultures, and find ways to create workable partnerships that overcome previously irreconcilable differences. We are able to face suffering without wilting, and surrender the need to sugarcoat difficult circumstances, harden our hearts, or cast a blind eye to intolerable or overwhelming incidents.

THERE ARE WAYS FOR US TO CONSCIOUSLY GARNER these treasures in our work with horses and bring them into our broader lives and others' lives. Peggy Nash Rubin's work in sacred theater offers a framework that helps create powerful experiences for people to explore their mythic lives. She frames our lives as a sacred play, in which we all are the stars of our own productions in the grand theater of our own times. Sacred theater is a way of looking at the world and at yourself that invites you to dedicate your life to a sacred audience, and play it fully with passion and power. When understood in this context, nine major aspects of traditional theater can benefit our way of living:

1. We create different stages for ourselves.
2. Everything that has ever happened to us is currently with us.
3. We incarnate many different roles in our own life plays and in those of others.
4. We want to express clearly and truly those things that require expression.
5. We will hold many shifting points of view throughout our lives.
6. Our stories are ongoing and part of a vast story of life on earth.
7. No drama works without conflict and acknowledgment that the greater the stakes, the greater the drama.
8. The essence of theater is a celebration of life.

9. The holy purpose of one's life play is to entertain the sacred audience, who is possibly unseen, unknown, and unknowable.

Within this framework, we can explore the roles we play, including the starring role in our own lives as well as the support we provide other sacred players. We are the playwright, director, composer, choreographer, designer, and producer, as well as leading actor, in this spectacular, magnificent, award-winning production of a lifetime.

Rubin explains the benefits of understanding ourselves as sacred players:

> Being an adequate actor in even a modest play takes courage, training, commitment, laughter, and a willingness to live and work within a community of others. The same is true for your role as the star in your own life. You remember how much courage it takes to live as a human being, and you learn to honor that courage. You train yourself to be more aware. You add to your expressive skills — vocal, physical, facial. You welcome your natural creativity and ability to devise and embrace new ideas. You focus your attention so that your body and mind become more alive.
>
> You are willing to recognize and study not only the many roles you play in your own life, but also the infinity of parts you perform in others' lives: lover, best friend, enemy, walk-on, bit player, stunt player, stand-in, cameo, designer, sometimes director, sometimes even playwright. This awareness of the importance of your roles in other people's lives helps you play them with greater verve and delight, deepens relationships, and generally makes life richer.[1]

When we travel the pathways of our own hero's journey, it helps to enhance our participation in that journey with the powers of sacred theater. The point here is not to view ourselves as any kind of celebrity. Rather, we can more effectively take the leading role in the mythic tale of our lives when we incorporate the powers of sacred theater and undergird our mythic dramas with the horse as one of our fellow players.

THE ESSENCE OF SACRED THEATER lies in celebrating all aspects of life. This implies that difficult work is often required to face painful aspects of our lives and give them full expression. Celebration encourages us to fully embrace and move through the pain and tragedy of our lives, knowing that those times are as important in our lives as the joyful times. This leads us to the power of ritual, which allows us to intentionally incorporate celebration in our daily lives so that it energizes our mythic journey in all its various forms. We can engage in ritual scenarios to empower any number of creative purposes, such as bolstering our intention to start a new project or revitalize an old one that's lost its energy, exploring the meaning and purpose of our lives during a dark time, or celebrating an occasion with high hilarity. We live with a variety of less-than-sacred rituals every day. We brush our teeth regularly, take a walk, and have regular meals. Starbucks has cashed in on the ritual of our daily cup of coffee. We find ways to celebrate special occasions such as birthdays and anniversaries, or significant landmark events such as marriages and graduations. All these celebrations are accompanied by familiar rituals that, at their best, lend the structures for us to deeply experience the event's significance, to ground it inside our hearts and minds as a piece of the sacred theater of our lives.

In today's fast-changing world, it is easy to feel immobilizing confusion and anxiety when, after deciding on a new direction, we find ourselves still shackled to old ways of being. In the hero's journey, the protagonist is often stuck at the threshold of a new realm. Clothed as dragons or monsters in mythic apparel, the guardians at the gate often show up in our own lives as doubts or resistances holding us hostage to hesitancy or half-hearted entry into our mythic lives. Rituals speak to the parts of the brain that are slow to change, the more ancient parts that keep us safe in learned routines but can also hold us back.

This was helpful for me to understand when experiencing the

breakup of my marriage after twenty-eight years. Even though I had firmly concluded that divorce was the best path for myself and my husband, a part of me yearned for the old relationship, regardless of my thoughts to the contrary. I was caught between conflicting aspects of myself, mourning the loss of someone whom I had previously considered a life partner, yet wanting to move freely into a better life for us both. I realized that a relationship such as ours implied a cellular bonding with another, a physical union that the primitive brain does not easily surrender. That part of the brain does understand ritual, however. My husband and I decided to have a divorce ceremony with a few close friends in attendance. Their role as audience to that piece of sacred theater helped augment the freeing effects of the ceremony, which was very brief but potent. As a culmination to months of sorrow and struggle, it was exhilarating to speak the words, "I release you from your vows of marriage and send you on your way into a new future."

Creating such rituals can help in all kinds of endeavors. When a friend of mine wants to lose weight, she knows that an important part of her brain responds to visual cues, so she creates a little ritual: she makes a list of numbers, one to ten, and posts it on her refrigerator. As her eating habits become reorganized around this endeavor and she loses weight, the ritual is to cross off one or more of the numbers as pounds are lost. It works for her.

Similarly another friend copes ritually with writer's block by creating a storyboard of herself writing. She has a page with small, empty squares, seven across and four down, similar to a month's calendar. She takes three of those sheets at a time, three months' worth, and very simply sketches in each little square an image of herself at her computer, with pen and paper, or sitting with her laptop at a coffee shop. She prides herself on having absolutely no artistic skill in this endeavor. Yet she finds that the visual ritual of creating the form, and then checking off the squares each day that she writes, provides remarkable structure and motivation for a task to which she is committed but easily distracted from.

As I prepared to write today, I opened a box of objects gathered just for the purpose of starting important endeavors. It contains a variety of items I have gathered over years: little pieces of silk in various colors, tiny statues of things important to me, such as a horse and a dancing figure, a white feather from one of my doves, a crystal received as a gift, an oil lamp, a tiny chime, pictures, incense, and other items that I have collected. I chose them for their wide appeal to the senses of touch, smell, sight, hearing, and even occasionally taste. I also chose them for their symbolic power to remind me of what provides meaning in my life. The ritual is to create an arrangement of some of these items that will bring intention to the day or the project ahead. In this case, I chose a swatch of hair from my horse, Emerald, a feather, a green silk scarf, and some very old vellum paper with Latin writing on it. Because today I am writing at a friend's coastal home, I also chose a candle colored blue like the sky and water outside, so that their spaciousness might symbolically inform my work. The items are arranged close to where I write, and as I lit the candle, I asked for my work this day to reflect the intentions of clarity, purpose, and beauty that began with this ritual.

Such rituals allow us to shift consciousness, focusing with more of ourselves harnessed to our endeavors. People must feel safe for this kind of adventure, because, to have any transformative power, a ritual must allow the participants to take risks. They must feel protected from ridicule, disrespect, or any number of obstacles that may cause them to resist the ritual's power. Some people are afraid to travel into their own psyches in this way, afraid that the terrors of the heart may overwhelm them. It takes courage and a sense of adventure to play this way. It is up to individuals to take responsibility for their own safety, respect their own limits, and thereby ensure the safety of everyone around them. Besides making that commitment, it often helps to state to whom or what the work is being dedicated. Having dedicated one's life to creating peace in the world, for instance, goes a long way toward providing the strength to confront fears along the way.

I have found, too, that even people who, for whatever reason, do not experience an "aha!" moment when participating in a ritual can trust that they are planting seeds in their psyches that, with a bit of attention, practice, and open-mindedness, take root and are harvested at a later time. Potent patterns are laid in place to bear later gifts.

IN OUR WORK WITH TEENS AND HORSES, after several weeks' work with their own hero's journey, the teens are invited to create a short scenario about their lives, a sacred theater piece that draws its power from the principles of ritual. This is to be a journey ride, essentially a short ritual, a miniature version of the hero's journey up to this point. To harness improvisational energy and eliminate any concerns about polish and perfection, the teens are given fifteen minutes to design three elements of the scenario.

First, they define for themselves something that they fervently wish to achieve in their lives, either in the short term of the next few years, or the long term, some larger life goal. It can be anything they feel passionate about: a career goal, some improvement in themselves, or a relationship. In the past, students have chosen such goals as becoming a drummer in a band, learning to express feelings more honestly, marrying and having children, or becoming the first person in the family to finish college.

Second, they are asked to identify at least one major obstacle that stands in the way of accomplishing this goal. Again, it may be a characteristic in themselves, such as fear, laziness, or a need for training. The obstacle may be something in the outer world, such as an unsupportive family or a lack of funds. They are given paper plates to create a mask that represents the obstacle standing in the way.

Third, they make simple plans for a five-minute journey on

horseback that will take them past what stands in the way of attaining the cherished goal. That goal is represented by a gold-painted horseshoe, which they will take home with them to post on the wall as a reminder of the goal. Along the ride, they take the shield of personal power that they created in the previous session. They are bolstered in confronting what stands in the way by the symbolic power represented on the shield: the power of the horse in the center, surrounded by images of their strengths, hopes and dreams, fears, and allies. And in this case, each is partnered in this journey with a live horse who has agreed to help along the way.

We encourage the teens to enlist others in the group in planning their five-minute scenarios and how they will move past whatever stands in the way. They might attach the mask to a lunge line and ask two others to hold each end as they guide the horse to step over the line held a few inches off the ground. They might ask someone to play a brief game of hide-and-seek for the same purpose. They might attach the mask to a jump standard that they must approach on horseback and dismantle. Before beginning the journey, the teens briefly announce to observers the goals sought and what stands in the way. They may talk about how their little dramas symbolize finding a way to remove the obstacles by feeding the demons instead of killing the enemy.

I usually hold the horseshoe for the teens to receive on the other side of the obstacle that stands in their way. I often insert a surprise challenge at the end, to heighten the experience for the rider. For instance, a teenage boy who wished to become a drummer was asked to tap out a drumming routine on the pommel of his saddle before he was given the golden horseshoe. Another time, I ran away from the rider, challenging him, "If you really want it, then come and get it."

The horses participating in these activities must be calm and capable of enjoying the high spirits that invariably erupt as the teens ride to remove whatever stands in the way of their final goals. The horses remind the riders that they have allies all along the way, partners who must be considered for their own needs and their own potential to help, and who will make themselves known in the riders' lives in any number of ways. In the journey rides, our usually calm horse may refuse to approach the jump standard where a mask is attached. The rider must find ways to enlist the horse's participation that were practiced in previous weeks, communicating with the horse in a respectful manner using more than forceful kicks and single-minded determination.

It is important for all the teens, as well as any adult volunteers assisting, to understand the critical role of the audience in sacred theater such as this. Traditional actors will tell you that the interplay between them and the audience significantly affects the outcome of any particular performance. The script, the director's guidance, the long rehearsals, and the talents of the actors all interact with the particular individuals who come to sit and watch, often with little understanding of their significant role in the production. It is more than the audience's laughter at the right spots, its applause at the end, or whether there is a standing ovation. Highly skilled actors know that the entire performance is essentially an intricate dialogue between themselves and those watching, whether or not the actors can see the audience. The subtle communication back and forth is not even at a conscious level, but the actors know its effects. They know whether or not the energy builds, the timing is crackerjack, or there is a kind of sizzle in the intense scenes; and at least in part, those qualities are defined by the audience's participation. Once we become attuned to others around us through our partnership with a horse, we can appreciate how these dynamics apply equally to our own personal audiences made up of friends and colleagues.

Others who are not physically present may join the audience too. A traditional theater performance may be dedicated to an individual or group. In that symbolic way, the presence of those individuals becomes a part of the audience. Seeing our lives as sacred theater, we can consider who populates our audience and to whom we dedicate our lifelong performances. We can invite ancestors from our father's and mother's lines. We can invite friends, teachers, mentors, and children. We can invite spiritual allies. Then we can dedicate a particular performance or a particular time in our lives to one or all of them.

In the journey ride, the teen players starring in their own productions, along with everyone else present, are asked to be conscious of their importance to one another, whether or not they are the main performers, because they are members of one another's audience. The main performer is asked to dedicate his or her performance to someone or some quality, perhaps even requesting that some higher good be present invisibly.

The performances are rough and unrehearsed, and, perhaps for that reason, they generate high spirits for all concerned. The rituals etch patterns into participants' bodies and brains to create clearer pathways for attaining what is important to them. This is playfulness with a very serious intent. With the accompanying power of their audience, they invariably experience a moment of gaining the boon, accompanied by shouts of joy and a victory ride around the ring where they hold high the golden horseshoe trophy. Even the teens who, a few weeks previously, were distrustful and sullen are elated by the power of this moment, both in their own starring roles and in their support of the others.

PATRICIA WILKINSON, a riding instructor in Ypsilanti, Michigan, tells the story of teaching an eleven-year-old girl in a therapeutic riding program who stumbled onto the power of ritual to help her through a difficult time. The girl had entered riding classes to help with her emotional neediness. Shortly after she had begun riding, her family started to fall apart. Her father's alcoholism began to cause major problems, and her parents were considering divorce. At the same time, the girl fell off her horse, and because of the stress in the rest of her life, she arrived at her next lesson too fearful to ride. Patricia responded by bringing out one of the ponies reputed for his stubbornness. Her idea was that the girl could have some quiet time grooming the pony and begin to overcome her fear in that way.

Instead, after a short time grooming, the girl left the pony tied and entered the arena where she occasionally had ridden through an obstacle course set up for one of her lessons. She carefully took nearly half an hour building an obstacle course that suited her. Then she called together staff and volunteers to observe as she led the pony through the course. She described for the observers how the pony had met the difficult challenge of going over a cavaletti (a pole mounted on either end to lie about twelve inches off the ground), how he did not really like to go in and out of the cones but did it anyway. She verbally described how the pony met the challenge of each obstacle in the way.

For several weeks, the girl arrived at her lessons wanting only to repeat this scenario in a new form she created each week. At first, instructors in the program felt uncomfortable with this because it was not the usual approach when someone falls off a horse. Ordinarily the girl would have been encouraged to get back on the horse as soon as possible, to avoid allowing any fear around the issue to become entrenched. This girl insisted on another approach, and Patricia sensed that she needed to back off and allow the girl to continue creating this weekly ritual with her pony.

To complicate things, the girl's mother arrived at the lessons each week with the expressed hope that her daughter would get on with the important task of riding. The mother worried that her daughter was giving in to her fear and avoiding the inevitable. However, Patricia sensed that something deeper was going on. She asked the mother to trust her on the matter for a few more weeks, which the mother was willing to do.

So, for several weeks, the girl created a ritual for her pony in the arena that was slightly more challenging each time. Each time, she creatively dealt with the pony's characteristic stubbornness and created more-complicated obstacles. The pony was asked to trot instead of walk. All along, even though she did not explicitly say so or even consciously know it, the girl was retooling her own inner world. She used ritual to lead her back from her fear one step at a time. As she encouraged the pony to take on a new challenge, she brought courage to her own self, so that finally, after several weeks, she arrived at her lesson ready to ride. This time of ritual creation for her was the start of taking on many challenges in her family life and growing stronger with them by trusting her own pathfinding abilities.

ANCIENT GREEK COMMUNITIES KNEW THE POWER of ritual and sacred theater for healing. Throughout the Greek world, small communities were dedicated to Aesclepius, the god of healing. When people were physically ill or world-weary from difficult times, they traveled to one of these communities for healing. There, travelers were welcomed for a stay of days or weeks. They might meet with a physician for healing herbs, but it was just as important to participate in the rich sensory life of the community, so they attended theater and had a wide variety of other experiences. Comedy elicited the release found in laughter, and tragedy the purging benefits of bemoaning life's pain. They heard storytellers on the street, enjoyed massage for muscular release and deep relaxation, and took long soaks in hot springs. They walked in the surrounding fertile hills that were forested with fragrant cedar. They engaged in conversations with new friends. They watched beautiful dancers, and they themselves danced to the rhythms of live musicians. They feasted on fine food.

When they felt ready, when their experiences had brought some relief and balance to the body, mind, and spirit, the culminating event began. It took place in the central area of the community, the *tholos*, an enclosed, temple-like structure where priests attended the travelers as they slept, with the intent of invoking healing dreams. Quiet readings of poetry and invocations by the priests accompanied the nighttime hours, with incense wafting across the dreamers. In addition, nonpoisonous snakes were released to wander about, in the belief that they helped invoke dreams and in honor of Aesclepius, who carried a staff with a snake wound about it. (Still today, snakes wind their way up the staff of the caduceus, the symbol accompanying the Hippocratic oath taken by graduating medical doctors.) In the morning, the priests assisted in the interpretation of any dreams that had been invoked. If no dreams came, then the travelers returned to the richness of the daily life of the community until they felt ready once again to invoke dreams whose guidance would accompany them home.

Interestingly, the mythic framework for the Aesclepian communities rested on the story of Chiron, a centaur who was an exception to his wild, warlike comrades and immortal because his father was Kronos, a Titan. Chiron was a musician, oracle, philosopher, and wise teacher to Jason, Achilles, and other heroes of the Greek world. He instructed their bodies in the skills of archery and other arts, while also attending to their minds and spirits in the search for their own destinies. Unlike his fellow raucous, Dionysian centaurs, he shared his intricate knowledge of surgery, incantations, and the healing properties of plants with Aesclepius, who founded the long tradition of healing communities in the Greek world.

Chiron was described as half horse, half man, probably from a race of shaggy, small men living in the hills who, at a distance, appeared to merge with the equally shaggy ponies carrying them about. Because his student, Herakles, accidentally wounded him, Chiron was destined to roam around, seeking an end to his immortality and endless suffering. In his attempt to ease his own suffering, he gained vast wisdom about the healing arts.

Carl Jung used Chiron's story to demonstrate the role of the wounded healer as an archetypal pattern, wherein many of mankind's greatest healers throughout history have demonstrated remarkable skill in healing others because of their own primal wounding. It is interesting to consider the idea that today so many people continue the tradition and ride their horses, Chiron-like, to a better future in therapeutic riding settings. Even outside of those settings, we can claim that high purpose for Earth and ourselves as we ride our horses on her hills and trails, allowing our Chiron selves — the self intimately partnered with a horse — to develop our capacities to meet the sometimes intimidating challenges before us. Here is a way for you to enact a piece of your own sacred theater with a horse playing a role alongside you as a powerful, Chiron-like friend.

TRY THIS
Journey Ride to Your Heart's Desire

You can create your own journey ride, a ritual ride to empower yourself for addressing issues in your own life. When you take a ride like this, you draw on powerful mythic patterns in your life, giving them ritual form so that they may begin to more openly pattern your day-to-day life. While it is best to avoid taking these experiences lightly, it is actually important to approach them with a lighthearted attitude. They allow you to rehearse the gaining of the boon, and they sometimes can be an extremely powerful event, a boon in themselves.

GOALS
- Experience the power of the horse as a partner on your life journey.
- Empower yourself to attain an important goal.
- Practice creating rituals that apply to your own situation.

PREPARATION AND EQUIPMENT
- Pen or marker
- Horse in halter and lead rope (or tacked up for riding)

- Small stone
- Five to ten leaves from a tree

For this activity you will work with a horse in a defined area such as an arena, a paddock, or even an area of a pasture. This activity is effective either individually or with a group. Even if you perform it individually, it often helps and empowers the participant to have others stand as witnesses, who take the role of an audience.

Time: Forty-five minutes

Take a few minutes to think about what aspect of your life speaks to your heart and calls you into the future. It may be a perfect job that you wish to have. It may be simply getting clarity about what would be the perfect job. It may be a desire to follow a yearning you have of any kind — to form a relationship with another person, to resolve a conflict with a coworker or family member, to heal a health issue that has your attention, to find a way to engage in effective peace efforts, or to resolve some dispute in your community. For the purposes of this activity, it should be something that you feel passionate and energetic about, something with a lure of becoming.

Gather five to ten leaves and write on them anything that you anticipate standing in your way between now and when you attain your goal. It may be your own apathy, difficult people, or lack of money — any inner or outer roadblocks that you anticipate blocking your achieving this goal. Look at the past and see what slowed you down or completely blocked you in other circumstances. Write your fears. List the unknowns, if you wish. If you can write one phrase that includes a whole batch of others, then do so. (Take ten to fifteen minutes.)

If others participate, then choose a partner and share with each other what stands in the way of your heart's desire. Be succinct in sharing, and focused in listening. (Take ten minutes.)

Then walk about the middle area of the arena and scatter the leaves, so that each leaf is placed several feet apart.

In your surroundings find a rock that appeals to you, something easy to carry, and take it to one end of the arena. Holding the rock, say something like this: "This rock, for now, holds my heart's desire." And then state your heart's desire out loud, even if you are doing this activity alone.

Then walk to the opposite end of the arena and bring a horse to join you. You can do this part either leading the horse from the ground or mounted, whichever appeals to you. However, sometimes it is easier to focus on something like this when leading a horse, especially if you are not an experienced rider.

First, stand with your horse facing the arena before you. Know that you stand in the present moment on this particular spot on planet Earth. Behind you in time are all the people and experiences that have brought you to this present moment. Imagine that they literally are behind you and that the future lies in front of you. Behind you lie the generations of your ancestors, for whom you are the prow of a ship, leading them into the future.

Hold up your left hand and imagine that it is connected to the line of the mothers. It does not matter if you do not know much about them. They stream back from your hand into the past, and their genetic coding gave you their specific gifts and traits.

Hold up your right hand and imagine that it connects you to the line of the fathers, far back into time for thousands of years. Their traits and gifts have molded your being as well. Stand to the side of your horse with which you sense your horse's role is most aligned — either the fathers' or mothers' side. If you're not sure, then stay on the side that is most customary for you.

Your horse will take this short journey with you as a mythic partner. He will represent all that you associate with the power of a horse — beauty, movement, sensitivity, and the larger-than-life horses who have populated your imagination. He will also be your partner in a very down-to-earth way, whom you will lead and guide forward in a moment.

For now, hold the lead rope in one hand and hold each hand out to the side, remembering that on the left is the line of the mothers and on the right is the line of the fathers. Directly behind you are the experiences of your own life that you bring to this moment. Review those experiences for a moment. Recall what it must have been like for you when you were born, when you were an infant with such simple needs as food and nurturing love. Take a few minutes to review briefly each year of your life, the years that stream out behind you as you stand here in this present moment. There must have been experiences along the way that helped form this heart's desire that lies before you. Remember them now. Some of your own experiences and traits have stood in the way of your attaining your goal. Remember them now as best you can. For now, there is no judgment about any of these. You are simply honoring what brought you to this particular moment. Include here, too, important people in your life who have been significant friends, teachers, or mentors. Times of great suffering, too, are here. Say to them, "You happened that I might be opened and made available to something new in my life."

Standing here with your horse, now imagine that behind you are these three potent streams — the line of mothers, the line of fathers, and the years of your own experiences — strengthening you from the past, lending depth and power as you begin to walk across the arena with your horse. Invite your horse to join and assist you in the journey. As you move toward your heart's desire, symbolized by the rock at the other end, be aware that you are responding to the powerful lure of the future before you and are supported by a huge entourage of the past behind you. Beside you is a powerful partner who calls forth your mythic life, the hero's journey of unique and grand proportions.

As you step past the leaves, gather them up, for they can no longer stand in the way. They may represent great trials. At least for this moment, they are swept away by the tide of your longing and the impetus of your life to this point. Even if you are not certain that you can move past the block that a particular leaf symbolizes, pick it up anyway. In this instant you have conquered it. You are finding a way through. (If you have chosen to ride your horse for this activity, then you will gather up the leaves later.)

Notice what your horse contributes as you walk; notice his eye and ear, and keep him engaged by your body language and explanatory words as you go.

As you arrive at the rock, if you are riding, dismount and pick up the rock, claiming it for its strength. Take a little time to treasure these moments for their symbolic success. Holding the rock in your hand, feel throughout your body what it means to have attained your cherished goal; this imaginative enactment prepares you at a deep level for an important unfoldment in your day-to-day life. Let it sink into your cells and retool your psyche, releasing new intention, new energy for what lies ahead. Let it advise you what specific next steps you can take tomorrow that will begin the unfoldment. Let the beauty of the coming manifestations send waves of pleasure through your body.

Whether or not you have a clear experience of this is actually inconsequential. You are placing within you the journey to your heart's desire, which will begin to take root, grow, and blossom. Know that your horse has given his gifts of heart-centeredness and power to your journey. Offer him thanks for those gifts and his companionship.

If you were riding, now gather up the leaves and return them to nature. You may want to bury them. They will transmute from the blocks in your way into a kind of holy manure. As such, the leaves will become nutrients for nature's renewal. Be aware of the blessing, of sorts, that nature places on your life in doing this. This is also part of the world that supports your unfoldment.

Now spend a few minutes writing about your experience in a journal.

WHEN YOU ENACT ATTAINING YOUR HEART'S DESIRE in the context of your own life as sacred theater, you also enrich the mythic patterns within your psyche. You weave new threads into the fabric of your imaginal life. You develop a whole new context for your daily life that will ultimately lead you into the pathways of your hero's journey, bringing back home the treasures of gaining the boon.

CHAPTER EIGHT

MINDFULNESS IN EVERYDAY LIFE

Bringing Home Your Amplified Power

WHEN WE ARRIVE BACK HOME after a mountaintop experience, often we are required to deal with the maddening routines of life. Laundry has to be done, dishes have to be washed, professional work needs our attention, lawns have to be mowed, pets need to be cared for, and our families need our attention; all of these aspects of our lives may have paled to insignificance for a time. We may feel intolerably hypersensitive and irritable about what we previously regarded as a simple, even reassuring, routine.

At the same time we may feel a sense of joy and expansion from our discoveries — especially if we can anchor our new awareness by finding ways to honor the details of daily life within the broader context of our larger lives. Instead of feeling the glow of our adventures fade as time goes by, we can find ways for that sensation to permanently benefit our daily lives. Instead of wishing we were back on the mountaintop or indulging our irritability about what we would like to change from our new perspective, we can carry forward the gifts of our journey and integrate them into our daily lives.

One way to do this is by practicing mindfulness during our ordinary tasks. With mindfulness a person promotes intentional awareness of his or her thoughts and actions in the present moment, without attaching any judgment to those thoughts. Although this practice was initially associated with Buddhism and sitting meditation, many Western psychotherapists, as well as several hundred hospitals, have adopted it for its healing benefits. In addition, a number of research studies funded by the National Center for Complementary and Alternative Medicine are currently focusing on the benefits of mindfulness.

The traditional practice of mindfulness meditation is to focus on your breath, following it in and out. On the in-breath, you can imagine energy moving up your back and above your head. On the out-breath, the energy moves down the front of your body to your belly. Focusing on the breath's circular pattern becomes like an anchoring tether bringing you back to the present moment.

By residing in the present moment, you begin to notice interesting things about both the inner and outer aspects of reality. Thoughts will interrupt your focus on the breath — the ride that morning, your horse's willingness to move through previous hesitation past a large rock, the shopping trip planned for later in the day, an upsetting conversation with the boss, sorrow over a friend's illness, or plans for next week or next year. The mind continually chatters with commentary or judgment. Before long, this commentary can spread a fog over the gifts from the time spent in the realm of amplified power, compromising our sense of its power and promise. We can end up with only fond memories and some good stories to tell of bygone times.

However, by noticing these habits of the mind, we gain the ability to decide whether those thoughts have value. We begin to notice that the intruding thoughts have no particular value or substance. They are just thoughts. We can set them aside for a time as we go back to focusing on the breath. In doing so, we realize that the thoughts are not concrete reality. We become free to observe our own lives without getting caught up in the commentary. Even better, we become much more acquainted with ourselves. Mindfulness is a wonderful way to become a good friend to our own selves.

As we more closely observe inner reality, we find that happiness is not a quality brought about by changes in outer circumstances. Instead it is the product of releasing an attachment to a particular thought about an unpleasant feeling or situation.

Many people find that sitting meditation does not suit their active lifestyles. In fact, mindfulness can be practiced anytime and anywhere. It's an especially interesting way to make valuable time out of standing in a line or waiting for an appointment. Any activity can become the focus of mindfulness practice. A good place to start is by walking and focusing on each step in minute detail. Walking down the barn aisleway, you can slow your pace and notice how the right foot goes forward, the leg swings from the hip, the heel touches the ground, then the rest of your boot touches the ground as your weight shifts forward onto the right foot. Then the toes bend, the hip continues to extend, and your weight moves off the right foot. After a few steps of focusing on the right foot, shift to the left foot, noting each detail as you slow the pace. Then after a few steps, focus on each foot, moving your attention back and forth as each foot contacts the ground. Speed up the pace and then slow it down. Other thoughts will interrupt your focus, and it is important to avoid chastising yourself for those interruptions. Simply set them aside and return your focus to walking. Doing this for five minutes now and then throughout your day can significantly incorporate mindfulness processes into your day.

Once you feel some sense of how to do a simple walking mindfulness exercise, it helps to connect specific words to each step. Again, start doing this by slowing your pace, and as you take each of three steps, mentally say to yourself, "Yes, yes, yes." Then with each of the next three steps, say, "Thank you, thank you, thank you." As extraneous thoughts arise, ask them to step aside while you focus for those few minutes on your walking and your words. Now the fun begins. You can take this practice to your daily routine around horses: feeding them, cleaning stalls, sweeping the barn aisleway, cleaning tack, giving horses a bath, and putting equipment away. Our teens begin to practice these skills in the relatively interesting atmosphere of the barn before taking them home to routine tasks that may have more stubborn attitudes attached to them.

Perfection is not expected. This activity is just something to practice regularly for a set period such as five to ten minutes. As your mind wanders and other thoughts intrude, it is enough to notice this without scolding yourself, and immediately return to the practice of alternating, "Yes, yes, yes" and "Thank you, thank you, thank you." It will be easier on some days than others, but the practice is what is important. The practice is a meaningful way to befriend yourself, to give the same consideration to yourself that you give to others. You will find that you get intimately acquainted with yourself by simply noticing the thoughts preoccupying your mind every day. As you notice these thoughts, for this set period you choose to set them aside for the opportunity to focus mindfully during your tasks. You begin to create a new subtext for your outer life. Instead of allowing this subtext to be driven by essentially fearful or negative thoughts, you can begin to anchor your life in positive thoughts. You find that you have a choice. And the easiest way to start is through simple, routine tasks, so that they no longer are peripheral to the more important, dramatic times of our lives. They become meaningful by giving us practice in making even our daily work into an opportunity for something new in our lives.

Molly DePrekel and Tanya Welsch have taught mindfulness for

years in their animal-assisted therapy called Minnesota Linking In-dividuals, Nature, and Critters. They find that, for their students, learning mindfulness begins at the barn in the process of learning to work around the horses. The procedures for placing the grooming buckets in a certain location and for grooming and tacking up the horses all become opportunities for practicing mindfulness, even though they are not labeled as such. When mindfulness is lost, for instance, in the daily feeding and stall-cleaning routines, the horses often become reminders of mindfulness with a stamping foot, a nicker, or a kick to the side of the stall. "Pay attention," they seem to be saying. Come back to the here and now. Be present.

In one sense, many of the activities suggested in previous chapters have to do with practicing mindfulness. "Lean on Me" and "Listening to Your Body" in chapter 3, "Developing Your Imaginal Body" in chapter 4, and "Enhancing Your Touch" in chapter 5 are activities that ask you to empty your mind of extraneous thoughts as you focus your thinking on a particular activity. When you practice mindful-ness during routine daily matters, you are then free to choose how to incorporate helpful changes into your thinking and daily living. The gleanings of your mythic journey give fertile new directions for your daily life. You find ways to move away from past habits into something new. Positive change becomes more possible.

Our work with horses can often involve teaching them mindful-ness. Young horses, some breeds more than others, especially tend to react instinctively with fright and flight or fright and fight. A bush blowing in a sudden breeze will sometimes leave a horse wide-eyed and frightened, bolting for safety with little or no warning, often without heed to a rider's desperate attempts to stop the horse. Or if the horse lacks the ability to run from being confined in an enclosed area, he will kick instead. Disciplining a horse for this behavior with whipping or other negative reinforcement is effective only insofar as it brings the horse's attention back to the rider. A more effective approach is to bring the horse to mindfulness in ways that build trust in the rider and begin to instill calm for future situations.

Kari McGehey has a particular interest in rehabilitating rogue horses, those whose misbehavior has sometimes led them to be given to her as a last resort. Zeus was an extreme example of such a horse. Because of his large size, over seventeen hands, and his explosive Thoroughbred temperament, as a young horse he had fallen into a pattern of always being at odds with his handlers. He was hypersensitive to things in his surroundings, and would rear up and bolt at the least provocation. He was considered unmanageable by a succession of owners and trainers. When Kari received Zeus, she knew that her slim physique was no match for his strength, and she immediately began clicker-training him. Clicker training is an approach that pairs the sound of a clicker with an immediate reward in the form of a small treat. It begins with rewarding a very simple behavior by the horse, such as touching a bucket or other item with the nose.

With Zeus, it was the first time he had been approached with a consistent reward-based communication instead of punishment for his behavior. The expectation of punishment actually had served to escalate his tendency to rear and bolt. After just a couple of clicker training sessions, Kari was able to interrupt his habit of responding explosively to unexpected events in his environment. When she led him out of his stall to go to daily pasture turnout, she was ready with the clicker, and the instant that she sensed he was about to rear, she clicked. Of course when her timing was off, she had a fleeing horse to deal with. Previous owners had tried all kinds of restraints with Zeus, to no avail because his greater size and strength enabled him to win the encounter. Now, however, Kari simply clicked at the right time, and Zeus dropped his head and turned to her for a treat. She shifted his expectation of negative encounters with humans to a more positive expectation.

However, leading Zeus from the barn down to a nearby covered arena offered a new challenge. With many more distractions to set him off, it was weeks before Kari could consistently lead him even a quarter mile without a major incident. Finally, she decided that she was ready to ride him. When they were just over halfway there, Zeus wheeled and bolted to run back home at a full gallop, frightened and in full instinctual flight response. When he swung about, Kari was unseated and found herself clinging to the side of his neck. She knew that if she let go, she would fall beneath his hooves. She struggled to get back up onto the saddle, to no avail. With all the sounds of the wind and the pounding hooves, Zeus could not hear her cries, "Whoa!" or the clicking sound she made with her tongue, which she had taught him to respond to. Finally, though, Kari clicked at just the fraction of a second of quiet when all four hooves were off the ground in the galloping stride. It broke the pattern of fear and flight, and Zeus immediately came to a stop and turned his head to Kari, looking for his treat, as she slid her feet down to the ground.

Zeus will probably always have a tendency to overreact to things in his environment, but clicker training offers Kari a consistent way to teach him to become more mindful about his reactions. It breaks the hardwired habits in his brain that were escalated by punishment, softening them with another option: to trust a human's view that he need not respond explosively but can increasingly try another approach.

Similarly, my friend Kate, who found herself obsessed with fear of her horses during a stressful time in her life, practiced a form of mindfulness to find ways to restore her confidence. Instead of responding to her fear by turning away from horses entirely, she observed her thoughts. She noticed what triggered her fear and, like a good friend to herself, found ways to teach herself to replace those thoughts and feelings with more appropriate ones. You can practice a similar kind of friendship with yourself by doing the following activity.

TRY THIS
Walking into Mindfulness

Mindfulness does not need to address dramatic incidents to claim its power to enable us to live richer lives. It is in the quiet moments, the ordinary activities of our days, that mindfulness enables us to do the extraordinary, step by daily step. It frees us from our habitual ways of being and doing in the world, so that we can pave new pathways, seeded by the gifts from the adventures of our lives. This activity can help make mindfulness a part of your daily life by asking you to commit to twenty-one days of practice. If you perform any particular activity for twenty-one days, you have a good chance of setting a new habit into your body, without conscious effort.

GOALS
- Begin to experience the benefits of mindfulness.
- Bring more awareness and energy to daily routines.
- Experience the joy that emerges when mind chatter is quieted.

Time: Five minutes a day for twenty-one days

PREPARATION AND EQUIPMENT
None

Choose a way to practice mindfulness for the next twenty-one days. You can walk or do some other routine activity mindfully, such as observing your horse's behavior in the field or in his daily feeding. (If you practice with a horse as the object of your mindfulness, you may find some interesting and productive interactions arising between you and the horse.)

Set aside any thoughts that intrude upon those five minutes of mindfulness. The task is simply to empty your mind of everything except your focus on your chosen activity and the words that go with it. As thoughts carry your mind in other directions, simply set them aside and return to your original focus until the five-minute period has passed. Even if you succeeded in being mindful for only a few seconds, that is enough for that day; it is an accomplishment.

Regular patterns for both the body and mind are helpful. For example, if you choose to walk mindfully, mentally say, "Thank you, thank you, thank you" with one set of three steps, and then switch to saying, "Yes, yes, yes" for the next three steps. You may want to vary the speed of the walking by going faster for a few paces and then slower.

For each of the next twenty days, take at least five minutes to practice mindfulness in the same way as on the first day. You can vary the details of the activity you've chosen, but make the activity the same each day. If you miss a day in the twenty-one days, then start the counting over so that you do twenty-one consecutive days.

It is usually a good idea not to practice at the end of the day, because the practice often tends to energize and awaken you, making it difficult to sleep easily.

Once the twenty-one days have passed, decide for yourself how often you wish to practice mindfulness — daily, weekly, or whatever works for you. Make a mental note to use mindfulness more often when under stress, because an upsurge in mind chatter often accompanies such times, which can be exhausting. Practicing mindfulness allows the mind to relax and often find new, more effective approaches to a situation.

PRACTICING MINDFULNESS allows you to return to yourself so that your innate power emerges for taking on the artful orchestration of your life in all its complexity. Mindfulness allows you to stay present to the mythic journey that encompasses your daily life.

CHAPTER NINE

GLOBAL CITIZENSHIP

Bridging Multiple Worlds

RETURNING TO THE WISDOM OF THE BODY — especially by connecting with horses, which charges the process with mythic implications — can lead us to a deeper calling to significant work in the world as global citizens. It is a calling that arises from the body when we attune to its deeper rhythms, allowing them to lead us to our mythic lives. This process can trigger such a powerful awakening experience that individuals are propelled onto the mystical path, where union with reality becomes an artistic process. What was once the provenance of a few has now become the experience of many.

Historically, mystical experience has arisen in times of radical social upheaval and change. Consider St. Francis, who, as a young man, was imprisoned during fighting with the nobles of Perugia, experienced a severe illness while jailed, and was later ravaged by visions that led him to eventually build his own holy order of the church.

We are surrounded now with such turbulent historical events that sufficient wounding is forcing us to find new coping strategies. Centuries-held convictions crashing down and traditional ways deconstructing invite a deeper spirit to arise in mystical forms that allow us to take on an inner spaciousness. We are suddenly knocked off course, and start engaging with a new level of radiance, focus, and vitality. Some have said that such times are the single greatest accelerator of human evolutionary growth. Jean Houston describes it this way:

> A huge switch in consciousness occurs, which you are not prepared for. You are suddenly outside of the three dimensions. You feel like you are in a larger, ubiquitous universe, and you've shifted into depth consciousness. Everything is interrelated, founded on truth and beauty, part of a holy perfection. Normal time — past, present, and future — is a surface veneer, like special laws within the larger laws of time. Mindfulness is intense. You are alert to everything: the sunset, emotions between self and others. You move beyond a half-awake state to a new state, startling in its vividness. You say, "What planet have I arrived upon? I will no longer live in my previous diminished existence." It brings ideas, plans, and the easy momentum to go out and do it. There's a recruitment of more brain function, and it sends out a frequency that invites you to move into quantum mind. You welcome the blossoming of springtime in your life, whose breezes blow away the outworn winter of old forms. This is a natural ability that we all have, a natural function of our mind-brain system, part of the equipment we all have but is latent in so many. We are being forced to cook on more burners now, to open ourselves to these latent abilities.[1]

I had an experience of this in my early forties. I was incredibly busy with my feminine brain's multitasking talents while developing many of the more masculine parts as well, such as raising three children, running two businesses, engaging in my marriage, and working in community development and the children's schools, among other things. The list was long. Part of my work was training three to five horses a week. I knew that every time I reached that synchrony of movement that we call "the zone" with one of the horses, in which the horse and I seemed to move as one being, something nourishing happened to my whole body, mind, and spirit. I especially experienced this frequently with Emerald. She reached her peak at about eight years old, and we were able to ride intricate patterns at a canter in the wide polo fields at my horse operation in San Antonio. I craved the times when it all came together in those moments of perfect connection, when I only had to think of a turn on the haunch and she would immediately spin about. Or she would leap forward from a standstill into a gallop with just a slight shifting of my weight.

Previously I had spent many years away from this kind of intimate connection with myself that horses facilitated, when pursuing work in a more masculine environment in college and when my children were infants. But for the past eight years, I had returned to teaching and training, partly in an effort to reconnect with a broader palette of myself. After several years, a sense of restlessness began to emerge that led me into the therapeutic riding field. However, one of the pathways of my journey at that time led me more deeply into my own body, providing another one of the adventures along the way. At a workshop one weekend, in the process of learning to develop the power of my imaginal body, I experienced a waking dream, or vision, that rocked me to the core. It was completely unlike anything I had experienced before. I felt visited by a winged, feminine being who lent me her wings to embrace the world. I experienced light rushing into my body from above, just as another energy arose from the ground; the two energies met at my heart, causing an explosion of sorts, a wild expansion of creativity and energy throughout my whole being. That heart energy expanded my own being and poured through my hands to offer some relief for all of the peoples' suffering on the blue planet I held in my winged arms.

I had sought a new source of energy for my work, and suddenly I was inundated with creative ideas. I could hardly sleep for a week. It was exciting for a couple of days, and then it became frightening. I realized why people might call an experience like that a hallucination and write it off as something to be forgotten. I was tempted to do so. But I also knew that I had asked for something, and an answer had come. Was I just going to toss it away because it was bewildering and strange? I settled into finding a way to assimilate this bizarre experience and take steps to understand it.

Over the next few years I continued to listen to my body, as Emerald continued to teach me through experiences of riding as one with her. As I became more attuned to my body, I had other experiences of this sort. I found a supportive community of people for understanding such occurrences. At first I thought this community could provide some answers about these experiences and what they were directing me to do, but I soon realized that it was up to me to find those answers within myself, to find my own way with the community's support and friendship, as well as the support of my horses.

The next dream of this sort awakened me in a panic one night, at first leaving me unable to recall the dream. After several minutes, though, I was able to slow my breathing, and I remembered. I dreamed that all the people in the world had a pattern for their lives, represented by a playing board such as a child's board game. My playing board was the Chartres Cathedral labyrinth, and I noticed that the southeast quadrant had no game characters, while the other quadrants did have them. Suddenly my father, who had died when I was twenty-one years old, appeared, passionately and tearfully pleading with me, "Complete the pattern." It was in response to his plea that I was jolted wide awake, panic-stricken. At the time I had no idea what my father had referred to, but my body was on fire with the commission that he had given me.

Seized by the urgency of this plea, I was unable to sleep for the next two nights. At a friend's suggestion, I made an appointment for a massage, hoping it would help me relax. Instead, as the massage therapist began by holding my feet, I started breathing rapidly and experienced a massive surge of energy up through my back and out my arms, hands, and fingers. I could see beams of energy and light radiating out through my fingers. I directed my hands to the sky, which seemed to offer unlimited distance for the energy to surge and dissipate. I imagined this energy even extending up to the stars. But that was not far enough; it had to go beyond the stars. Finally an image revealed that the energy had come to some place that was intensely dark, a kind of dazzling darkness. Even though it was pitch black, I was aware of an overwhelming power held in the darkness. I knew that if that energy came back into my body, it would be entirely too much for any human body to tolerate. But I also knew that I was supposed to bring the energy back down. I don't know how I knew this; the story unfolded from some place deep inside me, with a certainty that came from an unknown place.

I saw the energy start to come down to me, but it stepped down into something manageable, a form that took shape in front of me. I began to see a feminine figure forming from the light and energy, and although much of the rest of her became clear, her face did not, even though I strained to see it. Then, she slipped into my body through my right hand. I immediately began to reach to the left, seemingly seeking someone or something that needed this energy. I felt as if I were reaching back through time or, more accurately, reaching outside of time. Eventually I saw an old woman crouched down and near death. Although I had to argue with her, I finally convinced her to take the energy, which immediately vitalized her. Her gratitude moved me to invite her to come into my own space and time, so to speak. At that point my father appeared to me and thanked me for completing the pattern. I felt utter relief flood my body, and I was able to relax for the first time in several days.

I had much more to learn from this strange experience and others like it. I began to try to assimilate this new kind of experience into my sense of who I was. When I was a child my father had been important to me for his uncanny ability with animals. I have photos of him as a young man that show wild birds eating out of his hands. When, as a child, I took walks through our neighborhood with him, the neighborhood dogs rushed up to him and begged for his quiet touch on their heads as they wriggled with joy, tails thumping wildly. By contrast, the same dogs quietly and merely politely tolerated my childish efforts to imitate his touch. With him, the dogs were wild with joy, begging for more of his animal magic. It was he who helped me finally obtain my first horse. As I worked with these experiences of my father visiting me over twenty years after his death, I learned that I held in my body a sorrow from many generations of Scotch Irish ancestry that somehow asked to stop here with me. I began to notice how I held this sorrow in a way that no one else could see. I was good at hiding it, but it was there underneath. And it was time for it to end — now.

I felt called to carry on the legacy of my father's gifted connection with the natural world into my work with horses. It was more than something that simply brought joy into my own life. I felt that my work with horses was somehow connected to that initial vision I had experienced years before of holding and healing the whole world. I began to find ways to bring that healing work into the world. To bring that vision into reality, I organized and ran a therapeutic riding program in San Antonio. I trained to be a licensed massage therapist so that I could work more knowledgeably with my hands and with touch. I began to explore how to enact that vision in broader ways, as a citizen of the whole earth, that beautiful blue planet I had seen for the first time so many years previously.

I became fascinated with the idea that there are stories lying hidden that can be released into conscious awareness once we become acquainted more intimately with our bodies. I found that, when we allow our connection with horses to foster a deepening acquaintance with ourselves, and we empower that acquaintance by developing the imaginal body, these stories begin to emerge as part of our mythic lives. They were, and are, the stories that are patterned in myths, and they have their own strange and unique qualities, just as do the great myths of old. Myths began to teach me and provide a framework for understanding my own experiences, showing me how to take the next step along the way. Stories of Inanna, Sophia, and Athena enlightened my own stories. When I started to claim those myths as my own stories, I began to see my own life writ large. I began to step into a larger framework for my life and take on responsibility for more than just my individual time and my own family. With the challenges that face our planet today so clearly laid before us through the media, I was called to become a player, however small, in creating a viable future for the whole planet.

In our Western popular culture there is very little framework for understanding this kind of spiritual experience. In the face of daily demands, it can be tempting to label such experiences as pathological or extraneous to the seemingly more important demands of career and family. Yet, the trade-off is emotional and spiritual bankruptcy, and eventual physical repercussions. People who are led to intuitive experiences often feel relegated to fringe, New Age labels, or worse, to the population of the psychologically unstable. At best, they carefully hide or separate their disparate lives. Mona Lisa Schultz, MD, became aware of her intuitive abilities for medical diagnosis in college, but assiduously kept them separate from her medical practice. Then one day, at a book signing, a complete stranger asked her whether the numerous ruptured disks in Schultz's back and neck might have something to do with her split life. In the face of yet another ruptured disk, it took months for the doctor to recognize the truth of the stranger's query, but she finally began to integrate life as a medical doctor with her life as a medical intuitive.

I find it encouraging that the cultural life of the Plains Indians here in our own country embraced this spiritual calling for women and men until the past century, when various social forces nearly eradicated their traditional ways. In recent years women and men have been newly honored as healers, dreamers, and pipe carriers in the context of reemerging Indian religious traditions. Mark St. Pierre and Tilda Long Soldier collected many stories of women of the Plains Indians who were called to "walk in the sacred manner." In their tradition, "medicine dreams and callings to serve the Great Mystery were put aside until the active years of life had passed and the onset of menopause had begun. Until then, mothering preoccupied women's lives even in their subconscious landscapes."[2] This cultural tradition is supported by the current brain research demonstrating that the hormonal quiet accompanying postmenopause often allows women to engage in work of this kind with more emotional stability and focus, even though they may have been in training, so to speak, with dreams and other experiences earlier in their lives.

In this century and the last, Indian women often attended Catholic schools followed by college, which instilled cynicism about the spiritual path. This became a problem when the spirit world called. Yet many of the women heeded the call, taking their own hero's journey in trying to bridge their traditional heritage with their lives in our modern world. They usually had dreams but were unable to recognize the spiritual calling in them until later, when other events made it clear to them. In her thirties, Good Lifeways Woman bought a pipe as a simple wall decoration after experiencing unusual dreams, not realizing until many years later that the impulse had been one of many that eventually led her to become a pipe carrier, a holy woman with healing powers.

Even though everyone in an Indian community may be familiar with a medicine woman's role and the ceremonies that she conducts, nevertheless there is no clear pathway for someone called to this kind of work. In the beginning these women often expect others to step forward and instruct them, but they quickly find that most of their instruction comes from the spirit world, through their dreams and interactions with animals and nature.

As St. Pierre and Long Soldier point out, "No true Indian woman would want this calling or seek it without the right signs, because it might call for a lifetime of selfless service and, more than that, might place her in spiritual danger. Nobody can imitate this process, because the efficacy and power of the woman's dreams will be called into question by the community of the faithful every time she makes a prognosis or diagnosis or prescribes a treatment." Women who step into this role after menopause are not considered strange or exceptional and "are in essence no different from other women in the community except that they have an additional role to fulfill. Though the power of their ceremonies may command deep respect, in most instances their roles in family and community life are the same as those of other women."[3]

Dreams could go on for months and intensify, or they could dissipate and not return for a while. The dreams may be a call to perform a specific ceremony or set of ceremonies such as sun dance, kettle dance, or horse dance. In carrying out the ceremony, the dreamer purges herself of the impulses associated with the dream, allowing her to find ways of fulfilling her dreams in a role such as dancer or healer. Then the dreamer begins to build the particular ritual that supports her work. A healer might create an altar that is added to for many years over her working life, determined by instructions from dreams. "Bits and pieces of ritual practice used by the medicine woman come to her and must be affirmed, generally by multiple dreams and then, later, by results."[4]

In many ways, this traditional Indian culture embraced a wider expression of the capacities that people of our Western culture are just beginning to claim. Today we find a democratization of spiritual experiences that were once entrusted to special individuals in our communities and in more traditional cultures like that of the Plains Indians. As our scope of action and care expands and we orchestrate more worlds, we seek ways to meet dramatic new challenges. We are citizens of a world that no longer has clearly defined and distinctively different roles for men and women. We enter the workplace needing to develop latent capabilities and the parts of our brains that were less dominant in earlier, more gender-defined roles. We are called to develop and orchestrate vast new inner worlds, even as we orchestrate more-complex outer worlds.

Whether or not we experience this phenomenon in the workplace, we all are called to evolve new capacities when we see or hear increasingly vivid media coverage of issues such as war and global warming. A moral imperative rests upon us now for the earth's welfare. If we do not widen our perspective and see the peril in our imbalanced ways that jeopardize all life-forms on the earth, then we can only hang our heads when future generations look back in bewilderment and ask, "What were our parents thinking?"

In his film *An Inconvenient Truth*, Al Gore, as a modern hero living his life in mythic proportions, essentially tells a classic tale of this kind. Having heard of the trends of global warming from a professor in college, it was years later, after his six-year-old son suffered a serious car accident, when he saw what it might mean to lose more than his son. When his son nearly died, he realized that our entire world was similarly at risk, and a newfound passion was born for attending to the issues of global warming. He recalled his intimate connection with the natural world that he had known as a child working on the family's tobacco farm and faced the real threat of losing that natural world for future generations. He gained a boon during that dark time: a powerful imperative to enlist people everywhere to awaken to the risks of global disaster and work together to make changes toward creating a new and more viable future. He engaged in his political career with more focus on the issue of global warming, seeking to bring the awareness that he had found many years before. Now, however, more than an intellectual understanding of the issue fueled him. His heart was enlisted as well, and all the neural pathways of care, connection, and communication were activated.

The passion of this call helped him deal with his great disappointment at his loss of the presidential election by a narrow margin. Before long, freed from political obligations, he wrote and traveled all over the world with a spectacular visual presentation supporting the facts about global warming. Over and over again, in the face of multiple obstacles he became a man with a mission, who rose to the call to make people aware of global warming. The journey required him to orchestrate many worlds, both within and without, as he personally wrestled to find ways to more effectively communicate with those who did not wish to hear. He gathered around him more and more people who heard his message and took on its moral imperative.

WHEN ANY OF US ASSENTS TO RIDE into the mythic life, to do so effectively we need to join with others. As the community strength of the church has diminished, other kinds of supportive communities have arisen to meet the need, sometimes called teaching-learning communities. A large group is not necessarily required for this. As Margaret Mead is famous for noting, "Never doubt that a small group of thoughtful, committed citizens can change the world. Indeed, it's the only thing that ever has."[5] Weekend workshops and periodic teleconferencing abound for joining with like-minded others. In many communities there are numerous writers' groups, book groups, therapy groups, dream groups, and men's or women's groups for individuals to support one another's efforts to make changes in their lives and in the world.

The Millionth Circle Initiative, founded by Jean Shinoda Bolen, encourages people to gather for any of a multitude of purposes to "encourage connection and cooperation among their members and inspire compassionate solutions to individual, community, and world problems."[6] The millionth circle refers to the circle whose formation tips the scales, shifting planetary consciousness for the better. The phrase was inspired by the Hundredth Monkey Effect, a parable that has sustained social activists to continue their efforts when conventional wisdom has said that nothing (certainly not ordinary people) could deter negative forces such as the nuclear arms race between the superpowers or war efforts in other countries. In this phenomenon, once a critical number is reached, a particular learned behavior spreads instantaneously from one group of animals to all related animals in the region or the world. In India I heard the story that a few monkeys in southern India began to learn to pry the foil tops from milk bottles that sat on doorsteps after morning deliveries. Within a few weeks, monkeys in the entire region had learned this behavior, and once it reached a critical mass, monkeys in other parts of the continent, and even in other countries, suddenly had learned to pry the foil tops from milk bottles.

As Rupert Sheldrake posited, this phenomenon points to morphic fields of resonance strengthened by behavior until they reach a critical mass.

> The morphic fields of social groups connect together members of the group even when they are many miles apart, and provide channels of communication through which organisms can stay in touch at a distance. They help provide an explanation for telepathy. There is now good evidence that many species of animals are telepathic, and telepathy seems to be a normal means of animal communication.... Telepathy is normal not paranormal, natural not supernatural, and is also common between people, especially people who know each other well.[7]

Thus, when we join together with others for a common purpose, our actions and intentions have a reach far beyond the immediate circle of our company. In Sheldrake's terms we empower overarching morphic resonance fields, which I understand to be an aspect of the mythic patterns that we step into when we join with others in daring to live our larger lives.

As we have seen, horses are part of that company and offer their own special talents for becoming our mythic partners. They teach us skills of compassion and intuition as we ride into discovering our own unique stories of grand proportions. Together, we create a new morphic field. In the process, the horses taking part in this work grow into new evolutionary roles as teachers and healers. That's why physical therapists, occupational therapists, expressive-arts therapists, and psychotherapists, along with special-education teachers, corporate coaches, and other educators, enlist the talents of horses in every major city in Europe and the United States. Many of these practitioners incorporate other animals into their practices as well, building various kinds of cross-species communities for the benefit of their clients. They are creating a new morphic field, a new community that joins with others for building a new world.

Linda Kohanov detailed her own transformational journey with horses in *The Tao of Equus*, in which horses led her, and others gathered around her, on a path of awareness and healing. In discovering that horses are intensely emotional, intuitive, and intelligent beings, she found that they are also teachers because of their extraordinary ability to awaken intuition in humans while mirroring the authentic feelings that people often try to hide. At the Epona Center she has gathered people around her who recognize the importance of this work for themselves and others and are dedicated to sharing the work through workshops and training programs that have drawn hundreds of people over the past several years. She writes:

> I have noticed a definite strengthening of the morphogenetic field regarding people's acceptance of deep soul work with horses. The community growing around Epona is filled with people who are interested in strengthening their ability to move between the worlds, between humanity and nature, consensual reality and

mythic reality, between grounded experiences in the here and now with horses and spontaneous visionary experiences, as well as more formal shamanic journey and ritual/ceremonial sessions.[8]

YEARS AGO JOANNA MACY AND JOHN SEED developed a ritual experience that has enabled hundreds of groups to evolve into global citizens, whose primary community includes both people and animals. Macy and Seed embraced the term "deep ecology" as a key to the change needed in our world, especially in the face of radical alienation from the air, water, and soil, as reflected in the shredding of natural systems in the name of economic development.

> Although it is true that not many people nowadays believe that the Earth was created a few thousand years ago by an old man with a white beard as a stage for the human drama to unfold; nonetheless, this attitude permeates all aspects of our society, our language, our very psyche. Growing up in a culture permeated with this arrogant view of ourselves, we are isolated, separated from nature. As long as we maintain a self-image created in the matrix of such views, a shrunken and illusory sense of self that doesn't include the air and water and soil, we experience nature as outside our self and fail to recognize that the nature out there and the nature "in here" are one and the same. Moreover, we can't think our way out of this mess — the attitudes and habits are far too deep rooted.[9]

Recognizing that it was the denial of feelings that maintained the status quo, Macy and Seed developed the Council of All Beings, a series of processes that enables us to deeply experience our connection with nature, in our hearts and bodies. They recognized that all indigenous cultures, such as those of Good Lifeways Woman and the aboriginals of Australia, conducted rituals from a central role in their societies that affirmed and nurtured the sense of interconnectedness between people and nature. Together, Macy and Seed created a ritual that, first, encourages people to feel the pain of the earth in a safe place where the pain can be acknowledged, plumbed, and released.

Second, people are guided to remember their rootedness in nature through music, dance, and other activities. Third, they are given the opportunity to be chosen for a time by an animal or plant ally in the natural world, to make a mask of that ally, and then to speak for the voiceless ones. Many participants in this work have discovered that "alignment with our larger identity clarifies, dignifies, and heals our personal conflicts. We see that the pain of the earth is our own pain, and the fate of the earth is our own fate. The Council of All Beings empowers us to act on behalf of the earth, and gives us clarity and direction for this work. In the same fashion, it clarifies and orders our patterns of consumption, our needs for intimacy and support, our priorities for action."[10]

I have found such experiences of deep ecology with a horse to be especially powerful for people because horses partner with our mythic selves. Horses are especially suited for ushering us into the Council of All Beings, for being ambassadors for our global citizenship. In her work, The Eye of the Horse, Melissa Shandley builds entire workshops around mask making as a way to walk in the shoes of another being, the horse. These masks especially emphasize the unique visual attributes of horses resulting from their eye placement at the sides of the head, creating a blind spot in front of the horse's visual field and a correlated broader peripheral field to each side. Melissa involves people in the creative process of building a horse mask and then wearing it to evoke a shift from their habituated ways into standing at a portal for new information, more somatic information than most people acknowledge. Participants have the chance to see themselves as the horse sees them. Melissa elaborates, "As they deepen their bond with a particular horse or with horses in general, they find that they shift into perceiving on a core level. In addition to receiving intellectual and emotional information, they are able to shift their behavior because their point of reference for daily decisions is rooted in a broader perspective."[11]

TRY THIS
Widening Your World

When you open your life to the rest of our world, it can be daunting. It is easy to become hypersensitive to the violence and suffering around us. Maybe you cannot tolerate the extreme violence of many movies and TV shows, or even the news reports on the radio. Favorite murder mysteries may no longer be interesting, or at least must be taken in small doses and avoided just before bedtime. Emotions may run high on all accounts. It is important to honor such sensitivities without allowing them to shut down the awakening heart and mind. Instead of stifling sorrow and pain, it is important to allow feelings to be expressed in ways that their energies are brought to bear in creative forms. Then they essentially will energize your life path instead of divert you onto the side roads of avoidance and fear. Joining with others in some kind of supportive community is important for this reason too. One way to express such feelings and to engage with a supportive community is to playfully explore how these new perspectives can enhance your own life. You can play the following interactive game to widen your personal world toward global citizenship.

GOALS

- Widen your perspective on important issues in your life.
- Challenge your tendency to disconnect from nature.
- Recognize your fundamental connection to the natural world.
- Enlist new players in your mythic story.

PREPARATION AND EQUIPMENT

Choose an area large enough for groups of four to sit comfortably together in a circle facing one another.

Time: One hour

Choose an event in your recent past that challenged or upset you, something rich that still offers some emotional charge for you but that you feel comfortable sharing with others. One person will ring a bell, or use another signal, to designate two-minute intervals. It will help for the leader to give instructions for each step only when undertaking that step, rather than summarize the whole activity from the beginning.

1. From your own point of view, describe the situation to the rest of the group of four. All individuals in the group take two-minute turns, describing their own situations from their unique points of view.

2. After everyone has taken one turn, describe the same situation from the viewpoint of someone who was in the situation with you, someone who either opposed you or had a different experience of the situation than you did. Do this using "I" language, speaking as though you were telling your opponent's version of the same situation. Again, after two minutes, switch to the next person in the group, and allow that person to tell his or her story from the opponent's perspective.

3. Then take turns describing the same situation from the perspective of an animal as if it had been present at the time of the incident. Maybe an animal actually was present, but if not, then try imagining the situation from the perspective of a fly or an ant. Now imagine that a horse happens along and watches the event. Imagining as vividly as you can how the horse's perspective on the situation would differ from that of any human, speak as if you actually were that horse. Take a moment to step into the mind of this other nonhuman way of seeing your human event.

4. Imagine one of your descendants some 150 years from now looking back on this situation. Imagine that it is your great-great-grandchild who lives in another country, in

another part of our world, an entirely different culture. What is this person's opinion of your decisions about this event and your resolution of this situation? How would your decisions about this situation affect this descendant for good or ill? Speaking in that descendant's voice, tell how your actions have made a difference in his or her world.

Take a few moments to discuss among the group the insights and discoveries you have made.

IN OUR HERO'S JOURNEY there are times when we come full circle. Over a rich lifetime, the arc of the journey spans the many years between one's birth and death. Within that wide arc, though, over and over we find that some aspect of our lives becomes outmoded, providing space for something new to emerge. We experience many calls to adventure and trials and gain many treasures along the way, bringing them back to provide some blessing to the rest of our lives and those of others. Horses partner with us to ride into our lives with power, grace, and beauty, offering their mythic talents to teach us greater compassion for all sentient life and to allow new or forgotten aspects of ourselves to emerge for the benefit of building a brave new world of the future. With horses as our companions, we can ride into that world with the extended power of our mythic lives, experiencing the journey with greater joy, trusting our intuition, claiming our capacity for wise leadership, and stepping into our greater life.

AFTERWORD

Dark Journey of the Green Horse

AS I DROVE THE FIVE MILES to Emerald's pasture, I tried to evaluate what I had just heard on the phone: she was walking erratically in circles — not a good sign. "Probably colic," I thought, "but she has never colicked, so it must be a light case." My rationalizing, however, did not alleviate my anxiety.

Less than two days previously, I had finally decided, with the certainty that my veterinarian had assured me would eventually come, that it was time to euthanize Emerald after years of seeing her struggle with arthritis. That day, I stood by while a friend was given a horsehide drum for a dance she was to perform, and two things instantly dawned on me: it was Emerald's time, and I needed to make a drum of her hide, something I had never even considered before and, in fact, would have considered a bit macabre until that moment. In this context, however, I knew that it would be disrespectful not to make the drum. I then planned to spend some special time with her during the coming week.

TWO YEARS EARLIER Emerald had spent several chilly fall days barely able to move because of her arthritis. She was depressed and in pain. I had gathered friends one day to celebrate her life, in preparation for euthanizing her the next day. I braided her black mane with red ribbons and let her eat her fill of carrots from a twenty-five-pound bag. All afternoon, people stopped by with apples or more carrots. One friend read poetry to Emerald and chanted to her in Sanskrit. We thanked Emerald for her many years of teaching children and adults about wise ways with horses. Late in the day, after everyone had left, I sat with pen and notebook in the grass and asked Emerald for her words to me.

PRAISE SONG FROM VIOLET EMERALD

I would stop for a moment as a young horse
When we headed out from the barn to gaze far across the open field.
Yearning far into the future that lay before us.
Then I eagerly carried you forward
Away from day-to-day cares,
The hectic rush of the city,
The square rationality of stall and barn and bale,
Into the breeze,
Open fields of grass and gallops,
That clearing filled with a miracle of monarch butterflies,
Explorations into dark forests,
The joy of synchronous movement
Opening the hearts of wounded souls,
The Dance.
We gave one another all the gifts we have to offer
From our birthright —
You, human
Me, horse.
We are bridge-beings that way.

Now it's nearly time, but not yet,
For my light here to join with another light beyond this one.
Another sort of movement awaits.
You are welcome to accompany me —
Your spirit joining with mine in one flame of power.
Light! Wings!
There is comfort in your touch.

Then I wrote back to her.

PRAISE SONG TO VIOLET EMERALD

Praise to you, Violet Emerald,
Green horse of the earth,
Amethyst heart to wounded bodies and souls.
Velvet muzzle reaches toward me,
Ears and eyes are gentle, bright.
Your liquid, dark eye is calling,
Calling me to another place
Of deep-toned movement,
Punctuated by percussive hoofbeats,
Nostrils flaring.
Upon your back, becoming one blood, you and I,
We danced to rhythms of time beyond mind,
Dancing into another sort of being
The rhythms of grace,
Of yearning,
Of beauty,
Of silent, pure partnership,
Of connecting one species to another,
Of bridging worlds of differences
Through the symphony of movement.
Big eye,
Big heart,
Big back,
All carry me and you to that other
Dwelling place of heaven on earth.
Paradise lies between your eyes.

The next day dawned sunny and warmed into the beginning of Indian summer. I was surprised to arrive at Emerald's pasture to find an alert horse trotting about happily, still lame with arthritis but certainly not as incapacitated as I had seen the previous week. Thinking that it was the warm weather that helped her feel better, I called my vet and postponed euthanasia until the cooler weather would make his visit more appropriate. However, weeks stretched into months, and she never returned to that markedly depressed and painful state. Instead she began a slow and steady decline that plagued me with indecision about what was best for her. Dr. Tom Timmons advised me that one day I would just know. Somehow those words rang true, and I stopped fretting about the matter — until that weekend when, as he had predicted, I just knew.

NOW, AS I DROVE TO THE PASTURE, I told myself that she probably would be all right soon, allowing us the transition I had planned for the week. However, I arrived to find that she had suffered a stroke sometime in the previous twenty-four hours. As a result, she planted her front legs and stumbled in a tiny circle, repeatedly trying to regain her balance with back legs that she could no longer fully control. There was no doubt that, even though she was not in significant physical pain, her anxiety over being unable to control her body was reason enough to free her from enduring another below-freezing night.

While the vet tended to another emergency, I was grateful for the afternoon hours with her, to recall our twenty years together. I led her as she stumbled out of the pasture into an adjacent pen, where I could comfort her more easily. After a while, she began to push me with her head until I went to the side of the nearby barn. Then she stepped a few feet away from me and continued her perpetual turning, with her front feet planted in place. Minutes later she nickered and called for more attention. Over and over we played out this tender scenario until dusk, when she stumbled away from me and stood in the corner of the pen. Two geldings were across the fence from her on each side. The horses pinned their ears and tossed their heads for a few seconds, finally managing to establish comfortable distances from one another. Then they dropped their heads, ears relaxed, eyes soft. For the first time in many hours, Emerald stood quietly for ten minutes, seemingly supported by the triangular formation the horses had created. Then the vet and his assistant arrived as dark descended for the evening.

We walked to the end of the driveway, with Emerald stumbling sideways in the only way she could travel. The vet gave her the first of two injections, one that was supposed to calm her. From many past experiences, I knew to stand back for this procedure, but none of us had anticipated that Emerald would wildly swing her body around in a frantic attempt to keep her balance. I ran backward to get out of her way, but when she began to stumble sideways and fall, I was caught under her, and she rolled onto me, pinning me against the fence, belly to belly. I first thought I was fine because she was sedated, but we hadn't counted on the electrified top wire of the fence, where her right foreleg and hind leg rested. Emerald began to struggle wildly, and her back leg caught me in the chest and knocked me around like a rag doll, even as my lower body remained pinned under her. Later, I realized that we both had walked the boundary between life and death, performing a gyrating dance on its razor edge. I didn't have time to be afraid. I yelled to the vet and his assistant, "Get me out of here!" They each grabbed an arm and pulled hard, bringing me back from that precipice, back into life, as Emerald continued her own journey in another direction.

She continued to struggle wildly against the fence while the men disappeared into the darkness to get more sedative from their truck. While they were gone, I frantically tried to calm Emerald. It was only then that I realized suddenly that the reason she was unresponsive to our efforts was due to the electric wire she rested on. It repeatedly shocked her, overriding the sedative. I frantically called to the vets, who had been gone for what seemed like an eternity. They hurried over and confirmed my assessment, quickly cutting the wire and ending what must have been a torturous experience for her. She was still panicked, though, and the vets quickly injected her with more sedative. I noticed that the primary vet's right hand was covered in blood, and when I inquired, he reported that the reason they had been gone so long was that, in their hurry to return to the truck in the dark, he had slipped down a six-foot embankment filled with sharp, fresh gravel and, in doing so, had cut his hand and arm. This night was turning into a bizarre series of disasters.

In the next fifteen minutes, the veterinarians worked, and I calmed Emerald as best I could with my hands and voice. Finally, her body lay inert. My earlier thoughts of spending some quiet time with her were out of the question at that point. I was appalled that an act of intended mercy would end with such suffering. I knew that I was in physical and emotional shock and needed time to take care of myself and allow some form of completion to arise through the fog around the events.

Arriving early the next morning, I spent a few quiet moments with Emerald's body. I saved her mud-encrusted mane and tail hair. I made arrangements to gather her hide later, so that I could make the drum. Over the next several days, I tended the black- and blue-striped bruises that emerged zebra-like all over my body. I mourned Emerald's life ending in the way that it had. But I knew that much more would emerge from the experience. Shock held me in its protective cocoon. I waited.

FOUR DAYS LATER, I gathered with a group of friends for the weekend. As I sat gingerly protecting my bruised back, one friend asked me to direct an improvisational performance of the incident for the group, many of whom had not yet heard about it. Stepping up to the risky edge that improvisation always presents for me, I asked one friend to take the role of Emerald, another to play me, and another two to play the veterinarian and his assistant. Over the next several minutes, as we proceeded with our rough retelling of the events, an immense inner door opened for me, releasing the effects of shock from my body and shedding new light on the incident. For the first time I realized that I had been in a life-or-death situation and needed to thank those two men for saving my life. I noticed, too, the kind of back-and-forth dance that had emerged throughout that afternoon and evening between masculine and feminine dynamics, in particular, when Emerald had stood supported by the two geldings. I stood in awe that Emerald and I had been belly to belly for those moments, like a kind of birth trying to happen, recalling for me what it had taken to give birth to my own three children and, more recently, for my daughter to give birth to her first child. I was grateful to my friends that weekend for serving as audience for the event, allowing me to drop deeply into the process of healing the physical and psychological wounds, to drop deeply into the story that was unfolding.

I KNEW THERE WAS MORE, and so I waited. On Sunday, a friend brought to our gathering a legend from India that I had heard before but never liked because of its offensively barbaric nature. This time, however, I heard it with an "aha!" Great stories are like that — their layers of meaning emerge with numerous retellings, revealing the primal patterns of our deepest nature.

The story I heard that Sunday was this: In ancient India, occasionally a powerful ruler released a stallion for a year, allowing the animal to roam the countryside to celebrate and expand his kingship. His men followed and claimed for the kingdom any territory where the stallion roamed. After a year, the stallion was caught, returned home, and sacrificed with the intention that his energy would bless the future of the kingdom.

Verses from the *Rig-Veda* were read as part of the sacrificial celebration:

When you whinnied for the first time as you were born, coming
forth from the ocean or from the celestial source with the wings of
an eagle and the forelegs of an antelope — that, Swift Runner, was
your great and awesome birth.

From afar, in my heart I recognized your soul, the bird flying
below the sky. I saw your winged head snorting on the dustless
paths easy to travel.

Your body flies, Swift Runner; your spirit rushes like wind.
Your mane, spread in many directions, flickers and jumps about
in the forests.

The swift runner has come to the highest dwelling place, to his
father and mother. May he go to the gods today and be most welcome, and then ask for the things that the worshipper wishes for.

You are a victorious racehorse with the power to win victory;
go happily to the mares who long for you. Go happily to fame and
heaven; go happily to the first orders and truths, go happily to the
gods, go happily to your flight.[1]

Rehearing this poetry and the story in the context of my recent
experience, I suddenly knew that I was living my own, feminine version of it. Deep down inside I felt a redeeming shift taking place, as
myth dialogued with my own life. A new story emerged for me: Together, Emerald and I had spent twenty years roaming the frontiers of
our lives. She had been my first therapy horse in San Antonio some
fifteen years previously, when I shifted my work as a trainer and riding instructor into the field of therapeutic riding. I had named my
business identity, Green Horse Graphics, after her. With her, I had
roamed the frontiers of human consciousness, where I developed
the innovative, highly experiential program on myth and the horse–
human connection for teens in residential treatment centers and
adults in weekend workshops. She was the only horse I have ever
known who had headed more eagerly away from the barn on a trail
ride than toward the barn on the return trip. Together, over these
past twenty years, we had taught hundreds of children and adults the
way of the horse. The previous year, as Emerald had increasingly

struggled with the limits of her arthritic body, I had engaged in a new direction for my work, laying the foundation for taking it into a larger arena. Now, through this story, I was able to claim her death, with all its bizarre and tragic overtones, as a blessing for the future of our work, marking the end of an era that had become outmoded for us both. The drama of it suddenly became appropriate in my mind rather than tragic — suitably intense for the importance of the event.

That evening, partly because I am very attuned to my visual and kinesthetic senses, I felt a tangible sense of her stepping up to my side, sliding her head under my right arm, nuzzling me, and standing beside me for the journey ahead. In a distinct but subtle way, she now participates more powerfully in my life than she did for years. She is here now at my side, giving her horsey, marish input to this writing and to anything else I ask her about.

IT TOOK OVER SIX MONTHS TO MAKE THE DRUM out of a piece of Emerald's hide. I was grateful for a Canadian woman's instructions in preparing the rawhide and for help from a man from my hometown in constructing the drum; both of them recognized the sacred nature of drum making. I had never taken on such a project before, and from the beginning I decided to work on it only when I felt strongly drawn to do so. It was a physically strenuous task to scrape the hide free of hair, and when working outdoors in the winter cold, I quickly worked up a sweat. I did not treat it like any ordinary project in which my timeline was organized by a deadline imposed by myself or someone else. Instead, when I did not feel strongly drawn to work on it, I wrapped up the hide and protected it by freezing it, as I had been advised. I allowed the drum to emerge as the winter began to shift into spring, at the birth of the new season.

I allowed synchronicities to drive the actual work. For instance, initially I had no frame for the drum, though I had envisioned its size as about sixteen inches in diameter. I inquired in various places how to find a circular frame, but I didn't actively pursue the matter. Then one day, three months after beginning the project, I received an email from the person who, so many months previously, had loaned her own horsehide drum to my friend for her dance. She was someone I had only met and become acquainted with that evening, but I had re-layed how her gift to my friend had triggered my sudden conviction that Emerald's time had come. Amazingly, some three months later, she had cleaned out her garage and come across a drum frame. She had sensed that she should offer it to me. It had taken her a while to track down my email address, but she had persisted and, in her mes-sage, offered me the frame as a gift, if perhaps I needed it — perfect.

When the frame arrived in the mail, though, it was considerably larger than I had envisioned for the drum, and I wondered whether the piece of hide would stretch to fit it. As I laid the frame out on the hide, I was delightedly astonished to find that it was a perfect fit with-out even an inch to spare.

Fortunately my drum-making friend supported the process by making suggestions now and then, for example, that I might want to decorate the wooden frame of the drum. With such incidents sup-porting the process, I was conscious of the sacred nature of the drum's entrance into my life, and after six months it finally emerged into its current form.

Over a year later I read Louise Erdrich's book *The Painted Drum*, which chronicles a fictional story, based on fact, of an Ojibwe drum from North Dakota, a powerful yet delicate instrument that took a strange passage in touching and defining many lives. Elsie, a charac-ter in the book, described the traditional understanding about a drum:

> The drum is the universe. The people who take their place at each side represent the spirits who sit at the four directions. A painted drum especially is considered a living thing and must be fed as the spirits are fed, with tobacco and a glass of water set nearby,

sometimes a plate of food. A drum is never to be placed on the ground or left alone, and it is always to be covered with a blanket or quilt. Drums are known to cure and known to kill. They become one with their keeper. They are made for serious reasons by people who dream the details of their construction. No two are alike, but every drum is related to every other drum. They speak to one another and they give their songs to humans.[2]

I was grateful to hear this iteration of the living nature of a drum from the Ojibwe perspective, for it helped me to acknowledge the experience that has been unfolding with my own drum. I feel as though I somehow stumbled into a long lineage of those whose drums are "made for serious reasons by people who dream the details of their construction."

Today Emerald's drum gives auditory form to her presence, the energy of her blessing. Twenty years ago I was introduced to drumming in a dance class for which live drummers accompanied us on African drums. Our teacher started a movement for us to imitate and we soon found ourselves stepping into a time out of mind, borrowed by the complex, evocative rhythms of the drummers. Later, a Native American friend occasionally drummed out a Lakota song. I spent Saturday evenings with friends in a more spontaneous setting, where we drummed for an hour or longer late into the night. During those times I learned the drum's power to carry us to other lands of consciousness. In those places, body movement surrendered to the drum's power, evoking images and information about myself, a situation, or a friend. Until now, however, I never had a personal regard for a particular drum and its tone. But because of my twenty-year relationship with Emerald, this drum's sound, feel, and appearance call me into mythic time and space, with the heartbeat sound of the earth. It has led me out of writer's block on several occasions, so that I could access the place from which words flow. It has accompanied a friend who wished to dance into some new piece of understanding to solve a problem. I sometimes stare at the pattern of swirls on the drumhead, rawhide that once covered Emerald's strong hindquarters, and allow images to emerge Rorschach-like, providing a mirror to reflect on a difficult time, helping me find a path of clarity. I am only just beginning to explore its gifts.

OTHER TRADITIONS HAVE STORIES about the power of the drum. The Inuit people have a story, retold by Peggy Rubin, about a beautiful young woman whose father grew eager to have her married to an appropriate young man. He threw a party for her, and all the eligible bachelors arrived at the igloo and cavorted for her pleasure. Late in the evening two breathtakingly handsome young men appeared and lured her away. She felt overwhelmed with desire for these gorgeous creatures and happily followed them into the night.

As is often reported in such cases, the young men were not what they had seemed to be. As soon as they were outside the igloo, they picked up the skins they had left outside, wriggled into them, and became polar bears. They pulled the young woman with them over the ice and forced her down an ice hole into the bitter ocean. There they left her to the freezing waters, and soon the creatures of the sea came to eat her sweet young flesh. Nevertheless she stayed alive and conscious, and saw that one part of the ice floe above her was filled with light. She walked along the bottom of the sea toward that light. Soon the fish and water animals devoured every part of her except her skeleton, but she kept walking. Eventually she found a crevasse in the ice above her head, and pulled her bony self through it onto the surface again.

Remembering what life was like on the surface of the water, she promptly began to build a small igloo for shelter. As she fell asleep that night, she thought about what she needed: food; a safe, warm place to sleep; and skins and furs to cover her bones.

The next morning, everything that she had dreamed and imagined sat before her on the ice: a larger igloo and a recently killed caribou to provide both food and a warm robe. Each night she thought of what she needed for the next day, and each morning it appeared before her — except her flesh; she was still a walking skeleton.

One day while hunting on the ice, she noticed other hunters. They also saw her, and ran away from her in terror. When they reached their own igloo, they told their father (an old, infirm man who could no longer join the hunt) that they had seen a skeleton walking.

Now this was a wonder not to be denied. The old man considered; his life was useless, so what could he lose by seeking out this marvel? The next morning, off he went toward the skeleton's home. After long travels, he came upon her sitting at the entrance to her igloo. He was neither shocked nor frightened by her appearance. She invited him in and prepared food for him. They ate together and then lay down to sleep.

The night inspired the young woman. She requested that the old man make a small drum. He set to work immediately, created the drum, and presented it to her. That night she took the drum, blew out the lamps, and began to dance, while beating the drum with a stick and chanting magical sounds and songs. The drum grew bigger and bigger, and the air filled with the sound of its beats and the chanting.

When the dancing, chanting, and drumming ended, she lit the lamps and stood before the old man, suddenly beautiful and clothed in flesh. She looked at the old man, blew the lamps out again, and began to beat the drum and sing her magical song. When she stopped and rekindled the lamps, the old man stood before her, transformed into a young, handsome, and virile person. He became the perfect husband for her. And they lived well and happily ever after.

THIS STORY ECHOES AN UNEXPECTED PATH of Emerald's blessing for my friend who took Emerald's role in our improvisational scenario after her death. By interesting coincidence, she also happened to be the dancer given the horsehide drum when I prophetically intuited that Emerald's time had come. At the time of these events, and un-known to any of us then, my friend was beginning a courageous battle with breast cancer that had spread to bone cancer. Months later, when Emerald's hide returned from the tanning process, my friend requested that it stay with her each night as a healing blanket during her battle with cancer. Emerald's curly, long, winter-brown hair and fragrant, creamy hide covered my friend each night with a greening power that became emotionally critical for her return to health through the rigors of chemotherapy. The drum, too, spent several weeks with her. The calm that had made Emerald such an effective mount for young or disabled riders anchored my friend through many fearful nights. During those nights when terror threatened to overwhelm her, the hide provided what she calls "Emerald dream-ing," comfort that, like a starry sky, held her safely beneath, so that she could emerge into the next day with the courage needed to persist in the treatment that finally freed her of cancer. It helped her stay connected with the larger world of wildness and nature in the Grand Tetons of Wyoming, which had always empowered her as a dancer. It gave her a sense of how to continue dancing with this most chal-lenging experience of her life. The drum's heartbeat rhythm helped sustain that dance too.

My own work with Emerald lies in those boundaries between the seen and unseen worlds that she and I cohabit. It's now time for me to claim my own queendom, so to speak, as the Indian myth of the horse sacrificed for the future of the kingdom revealed to me that day. In a subtle but spectacular manner, Emerald continues teaching me and others that we are members of a powerful, emerging part-nership of all living beings that is developing to benefit our planet's future. Through her, and other animals like her, we learn to trust our ability to live life joyfully despite troubling times, accompanied and supported by more than we ever before thought possible. With horses like her, who populate our imaginations as well as our day-to-day lives, we can explore the mythic dimensions of our lives. These experiences open new territory for our centuries-long partnership with horses, and support the emerging partnership of all living beings — a partnership necessary for our planet's future. By learning to partner with horses, we can gain the skill of compassionate leadership, hone our intuitions, and develop effective but sensitive communication styles and wiser awareness of others. We can develop our latent capacities to deal with challenging times. Our efforts are strengthened for making positive changes in the world — in classrooms, boardrooms, and other situations of human decision making around the world — as we ride into our mythic lives.

ACKNOWLEDGMENTS

DURING MY TWENTY YEARS OF WORK with myth and the horse–human connection, I have been fortunate to spend nearly ten years as a full-time therapeutic-riding instructor and executive director, joining with students, instructors, administrators, volunteers, and some special horses to form a heart-centered partnership between horses and humans. NARHA and the Equine Facilitated Mental Health Association have provided me an invaluable collegial network supporting this work. I have been equally fortunate to have had the opportunity to study and work closely with Jean Houston and her Mystery School, and especially Peggy Nash Rubin and her Center for Sacred Theatre, where I am part of a rich, worldwide community of like-minded others, seeking to bring forth positive and innovative new forms for the future of our world. I am grateful for their teachings and friendship, which are cornerstones for my life and my work.

My gratitude also extends to my family, Matthew, Nathan, Lauren, and Tom, who constantly rekindle my hope for the future through their courageous and loving ways; and my circles of women — the Veggies, the Sparta Dancers, the Catalytics, the WSR, and Dream Group — where I dwell and grow in a profound sisterhood of the feminine mysteries. In all of these associations, I have known countless other individuals who have answered an amazing variety of high calls to adventure, including my current riding buddies Julie Campbell and Pat Super. This book is dedicated to their courage, their stories, and the mythic companions who accompany them.

I APPLAUD THE EXPERTISE AND ENTHUSIASM of my editor, Jason Gardner, and the staff of New World Library, whose dedication to publishing books that change people's lives is a bright beacon of possibility in a world increasingly preoccupied with electronic media.

NOTES

CHAPTER 1
THE POWER OF MYTH FOR YOUR LIFE

1. Jean Houston, *The Search for the Beloved* (Los Angeles: Jeremy P. Tarcher, Inc., 1987), 31.

2. Pattiann Rogers, *Firekeeper: Selected Poems*, revised and expanded ed. (Minneapolis, MN: Milkweed Editions, 2005), © Pattiann Rogers. Reprinted with permission from Milkweed Editions.

CHAPTER 2
UNIVERSAL PATTERNS FOR YOUR LARGER LIFE PURPOSE

1. Jean Houston in private conversation.

2. William Hutchinson Murray, *The Scottish Himalayan Expedition* (London: J. M. Dent and Sons Ltd., 1951).

3. Louann Brizendine, *The Female Brain* (New York: Broadway, 2006).

4. Monty Roberts, *The Man Who Listens to Horses* (New York: Random House, 1997).

5. Tsultrim Allione, http://www.taramandala.com/pr_07_Kapala1 _CA.htm.

6. Jamie Sams and David Carson, *Animal Medicine* (Santa Fe, NM: Bear and Company, 1988), 53.

CHAPTER 3
HORSES FOR PARTNERSHIP AND NEW ADVENTURE

1. Julie Goodnight, online newsletter commentary, http://www .juliegoodnight.com.

2. Swami Nikhilananda, trans., *The Upanishads: A New Translation*, http://www.sankaracharya.org/brihadaranyaka _upanishad.php.

3. Jean Auel, *Valley of the Horses* (New York: Crown Publishers, 1982), 167.

4. Ibid., 168.

5. Ibid., 169.

6. Ibid., 170.

CHAPTER 4
ALLIES FOR THE JOURNEY

1. Peter A. Campbell and Edwin M. McMahon, *Bio-Spirituality: Focusing as a Way to Grow*, 2nd ed. (Chicago: Loyola Press, 1985, 1997), 64–70. Reprinted with permission of Peter A. Campbell.

2. All activities in this section are based on an exercise by Jean Houston, PhD, adapted from an unpublished transcript of a Mystery School session.

CHAPTER 5

ENERGY, COMMUNICATION, AND THE EXPANDED SELF

1. Rupert Sheldrake, "Morphic Fields and Morphic Resonance: An Introduction," http://www.sheldrake.org/Articles&Papers /papers/morphic/morphic_intro.html.

2. The Compassionate Listening Project, P.O. Box 17, Indianola, WA 98342, (360) 297-2280, http://www.compassionate listening.org.

3. Jean Houston's Social Artistry, http://www.jeanhouston.org.

4. Morgan Llewellyn, *The Horse Goddess* (New York: Simon and Schuster, 1982), 39.

5. Ibid., 218.

6. Ibid., 219.

7. Ibid., 219–21.

8. This activity is from the author's practice of the work of Linda Tellington-Jones, http://www.lindatellington-jones.com.

CHAPTER 6

SYMBOLS TO SUSTAIN YOU ON THE JOURNEY

1. Institute of Cultural Affairs, 4750 N. Sheridan Road, Chicago, IL 60640, (773) 769-6363, http://www.ica-usa.org.

2. Carl Jung, *Man and His Symbols* (New York: Doubleday, 1969).

3. Gerald and Loretta Hausman, *The Mythology of Horses: Horse Legend and Lore Throughout the Ages* (New York: Three Rivers Press, 2003), 40.

4. Clement of Alexandria, Stromata IV, 25, as quoted at http://en.wikipedia.org/wiki/Alpha_and_Omega.

5. Loretta Afraid of Bear Cook, Afraid of Bear American Horse Sun Dance sponsor and coordinator, in private conversation;

Oglala Lakota Nation, 1705 S. Maple Street, Chadron, NE 69337, (308) 432-3409.

6. Dane Coolidge and Mary Robert Coolidge, *The Navajo Indians* (Boston, MA: Houghton Mifflin, 1930), 2.

7. Judith Cornell, *Mandala: Luminous Symbols for Healing*, 10th ed. (Wheaton, IL: Quest Books, 2007).

8. Hyemeyohsts Storm, *Seven Arrows* (New York: Ballantine Books, 1979).

9. TeachingHorse, http://www. teachinghorse.com.

10. Denise Kester in private conversation (see also http://www .drawingonthedream.com).

11. Ibid.

12. Ibid.

13. Ibid.

CHAPTER 7
YOUR LIFE AS SACRED THEATER

1. Margaret Nash Rubin in private conversation (see also http://www.sacredtheatre.org).

CHAPTER 9
GLOBAL CITIZENSHIP

1. Jean Houston, in private conversation (see also http://www.jean houston.org).

2. Mark St. Pierre and Tilda Long Soldier, *Walking in the Sacred Manner: Healers, Dreamers, and Pipe Carriers — Medicine Women of the Plains Indians* (New York: Touchstone, 1995).

3. Ibid., 27.

4. Ibid.

5. Attributed to Margaret Mead, specific source unknown.

6. Jean Shinoda Bolen, http://www.millionthcircle.org/About/intentions.html.

7. Rupert Sheldrake, http://www.sheldrake.org/papers/Morphic/morphic_intro.html.

8. Private conversation with Linda Kohanov, author of *The Tao of Equus: A Woman's Journey of Healing and Transformation through the Way of the Horse* (Novato, CA: New World Library, 2001).

9. John Seed, *The Council of All Beings*, http://www.rainforestinfo.org.au/deep-eco/council.htm.

10. Ibid.

11. Melissa Shandley, in private conversation (see also http://www.theeyeofthehorse.com).

AFTERWORD

1. Wendy Doniger O'Flaherty, trans., *Rig-Veda* (New York: Penguin Classics, 1981), 89.

2. Louise Erdrich, *The Painted Drum* (New York: HarperCollins, 2005), 43.

INDEX

A

Adventure Camp (San Antonio, TX), xix–xx, xxi, 54–55
adventure games
    Citizens in the Local Community, 39–40
    Heroic Tales, 37–39
    hero's journey and, 34, 36–37, 40–41
    intent of, 36
    Riding into a New Future, 41–42
adventures. *See* call to adventure; trials/adventures
Aesclepius, 141–42

affluence, effects of, 123–24
Afraid of Bear American Horse Sun Dance, 109–10
aggression, 48, 49
allies
    animals as, 125, 127, 173
    exercises for, 77–84
    in hero's journey, 18, 20
    horses as, 71
    inner, 73–76
    See also imaginal body
Allione, Tsultrim, 35
American Saddlebreds, xv
Andy (therapeutic riding student), 105–6

anger, xvi–xvii
animal communication, 170–72
Animal Medicine (Sams and
   Carson), 35–36
animals
   as allies, 125, 127, 173
   symbolic role of, 116–23
animal sensibilities, entering
   (exercise), 79–82
anthropomorphism, 46
antiwar protests, 108
Aphrodite, 12
Apollo oracle site (Didyma,
   Turkey), 122
Arabs, human/horse partnerships of, 43–44
archetypes, 12–13, 142–43
Artemis, 11–12
Artress, Lauren, 114
assertiveness, 48, 49–50
Athena, 12–13
atomic bomb, as symbol, 107–8
audience, in sacred theater, 138–39
Auel, Jean, 62–65
Australian aboriginals, 172
awareness
   boundaries of, 85–86
   human/horse partnerships
      and, 191

B

Bellerophon, 11
belly of the whale, 85, 97

Bible, 18
Bio-Spirituality (P. Campbell),
   74–76
Black Stallion, The (film), 18
   allies in, 20
   call to adventure in, 19
   gaining the boon in, 22–23
   return in, 23
   tests in, 21–22
   threshold crossing in, 20–21
body
   human/horse partnerships
      and, 31–32
   listening to, 65–67, 153, 162
   subtle, 73
   wisdom of, 159
   See also imaginal body
body language, 55–56, 68–69, 86
boon, gaining of
   in hero's journey, 18–19, 22–24
   in human/horse partner-
      ships, 130–31
   journey rides as rehearsal
      for, 143
   mythic life and, 129
   patterns leading up to,
      129–30
   See also return
brain, primitive, 26–27
breathing, focus on, 150–51
Brizendine, Louann, 26, 29
Buddhism, 34–35, 113, 150
Burn, Skye, 116–17

C

caduceus, 142
call to adventure
    birth as, 43
    in hero's journey, 18, 19–20
    by horses, 52–55, 62–65
    refusal of, 19
Campbell, Joseph, 17
Campbell, Peter A., 74–76
Carson, David, 35–36, 124–25
Celtic lore/mythology, 92–97
chakra system, 73
Chartres Cathedral (France), 114,
    162
children, horses as symbolic for,
    105–6
    See also therapeutic riding
    programs
Chinese astrology, 118
Chinese medicine, 73, 90, 120–21
Chiron, 142–43
Citizens in the Local Commu-
    nity (adventure game sce-
    nario), 39–40
clicker training, 154–55
collective imagination, 1
communication
    energetic, 65–68, 94–97
    exercises for, 57–60, 65–67,
    97–101
    human/horse partnerships
    and, 43, 44, 48–49, 60–62,
    138, 191
    inner source of, 85–86
    morphic fields and, 170–72
    nonverbal, 57, 60–62, 66,
    68–70
    subtle, xxi, 103
compassion, xxi, 55, 130–31, 176,
    191
Compassionate Listening Proj-
    ect, 90
competition
    adventure games and, 36
    author's distaste for, xx
    benefits of, 32
    destructive eventualities of, 33
    gender and, 31–32
    health consequences of, 31–32
    in horse shows, 52–53, 71–72
    in riding, 33–34
complexity, 24
conception, as hero's journey,
    27–28
conflict, 100–101
Cook, Loretta Afraid of Bear,
    109–10
cooperation, 51–52
Cornell, Judith, 111
Council of All Beings, 172–73
Cretan labyrinth form, 114–15
crows, as symbols, 117

D

dance, 173
deep ecology, 172–73

demons, feeding, 34–36
DePrekel, Molly, 152–53
depression, 21, 74
Developing Your Imaginal Body
     (exercise), 76–84, 153
Didyma (Turkey), 122
dieting, rituals for, 134
Dignan, Denise, 31
divorce, ritual ceremony for, 134
Dollar (horse), 49–50
doubt, 133
dreams, 127
     healing, 142, 166–67
     horses in, 117–19
     waking (visions), 161–64
drum, horsehide, 177, 185–88
Dually (horse), 61–62
Duke (stud colt), 45
Duke, Chris, xx–xxi

E

eagles, as symbols, 116–17
Earth, as symbol, 107–8
ecology, deep, 172–73
Eden, Donna, 91
email communication, 15
Emerald (horse), 161
     author's purchase of, xiii,
          xviii
     claiming death of, 182–85
     drum from hide of, 177,
          185–88, 190
     euthanization of, 177–82
     healing power of, 189–90

praise songs, 178–79
     trust inspired by, xx
energy medicine, 91
Energy Medicine (Gerber), 91
energy meridians, 73
Enhancing Your Touch (exer-
     cise), 97–101, 153
entelechy, 15–16
Entering the Sensibilities of Ani-
     mals (exercise), 79–82
Epona (Celtic deity), 93–97
Epona Center (Sonoita, AZ),
     171–72
Equine Facilitated Mental Health
     Association (EFMHA), 3–4
Erdrich, Louise, 186–87
Estés, Clarissa Pinkola, 12
euthanasia, 177–82
everyday life
     call to adventure in, 19
     gaining the boon in, 22
     mindfulness and, 150
     return in, 23–24, 149–50
     ritual in, 134–36
     spirituality lacking in, 165
     symbols needed for, 123–24
     tests in, 22
     threshold crossing in, 21
exercises
     Developing Your Imaginal
          Body, 76–84, 153
     Enhancing Your Touch,
          97–101, 153
     Entering the Sensibilities of
          Animals, 79–82

Exploring Your Imaginal
  Body, 77–79
Journey Ride to Your Heart's
  Desire, 143–47
Lean on Me, 57–60, 153
Listening to Your Body,
  65–67, 153
Meeting Your Higher Self,
  82–84
Walking into Mindfulness,
  156–57
Widening Your World,
  174–76
Your Shield of Power, 124–27
Exploring Your Imaginal Body
  (exercise), 77–79

F

fear, 87–90, 126–27, 155
Feeding Your Demons (training
  program), 35
Female Brain, The (Brizendine),
  26, 29
feng shui, 106
Foxfire (horse), 50
Francis, Saint, 159

G

gender
  competition and, 31–32
  hero's journey and, 26–29
  human/horse partnerships
    and, 29–31
  physical sensations and, 30

Gerber, Richard, 91
global citizenship
  deep ecology and, 172–73
  exercise for, 174–76
  human/horse partnerships
    and, xxi, 159, 173
  moral imperative for, 168–69
  morphic fields and, 170–72
global warming, 168–69
Good Lifeways Woman, 166, 172
Goodnight, Julie, 47
Gore, Al, 168–69
Greece, ancient, 141–42
Green Horse Graphics, 184
guardians, 18, 20, 133
Gunter, June, 114–15

H

handicapped, the, therapeutic
  riding programs for, xix–xxi,
  2–3, 40–41
hand signals, 68
Harry Potter books/films, 18
Hausman, Gerald, 108
Hausman, Loretta, 108
healing
  as hero's journey, 24–25
  medicine women, 166–67
  sacred theater and, 141–43
  therapeutic riding programs
    and, xix–xxi
  through stories, 182–85
  wounded healer archetype,
    142–43

healing touch, 91–92, 97–101, 103
herd behavior, 56–57
Heroic Tales (adventure game
    scenario), 37–39
hero's journey
    adventure games and, 34,
        36–37, 40–41
    arc of, 176
    complex modern life and, 24
    conception as, 27–28
    described, 18–24, 26
    gender differences in, 26–29
    in therapeutic riding pro-
        grams, 136–41
    treatment as, 24–25
    universality of, 17–18
    See also specific stage
Hippocratic oath, 142
Hiroshima, 108
hopes, 127
horseback riding, competition
    in, 33–34
Horse Goddess, The (Llewellyn),
    94–97
horsemanship, basic skills for, 55
horse masks, making, 173
horses
    anatomy, 56, 110
    anger toward, xvi–xvii
    author's experiences with,
        xv–xxiii
    body language, 55–56
    calls to adventure made by,
        52–55, 62–65

deep ecology with, 173
herd behavior, 56–57
as inner allies, 71
mindfulness practice with,
    152–55
as mythic creatures, 1, 4, 5,
    7–8, 9–11, 62, 159
rental, xiii–xiv
sentient nature of, 3, 48–49
symbolic role of, 104–6,
    109–10, 117–19
touch techniques with,
    97–101
transformative powers of,
    2–4
utilitarian value of, 4–5
horseshoes, as symbols, 108–9
horse shows
    boon in, 130
    competition in, 52–53, 71–72
    therapeutic riding programs
        and, xix
    training methods for, xv,
        xvii
horse training
    author's experiences with,
        xvi–xix
    clicker training, 154–55
    human/horse partnerships
        and, 88–90
    leadership in, 47–52
    mindfulness in, 153–55
horse whisperers, 44
Houston, Jean, 8–9, 17–18, 90–91,
    160

human conflict, 100–101

human/horse partnerships,
 122–23
 boon in, 130–31
 call to adventure, 52–55, 62–65
 as choice, 45–46
 communication skills re-
  quired for, 43, 44, 48–49,
  60–62, 67–68, 138, 191
 cooperation in, 51–52
 deep ecology and, 173
 exercises for, 57–60, 65–67
 exploring/studying, 55–57
 fear and, 87–90
 gender differences in, 29–31
 global citizenship and, xxi,
  159, 173
 healing power of, 189–90
 history of, 43–44, 54
 imaginal body and, 84, 89–90
 labyrinth-walking, 114–16
 leadership in, 46, 47–52, 68–70
 misguided expectations in, 46
 morphic fields and, 170–72
 mythic aspect of, 15, 176,
  190–91
 as sacred theater, 132
 safety concerns in, 55, 66
 in therapeutic riding programs, 4, 136–41
 "the zone" in, 160–61

humans
 complex lives of, 24
 myth and, 12–14
 nonlinear life patterns of, 25

Hundredth Monkey Effect, 170

Hyjek, Beth, 114–15

I

imaginal body, 161
 defined, 76
 developing (exercise), 76–84
 exploring, 77–79
 human/horse partnerships
  and, 89–90
 as inner resource, 103
 touch techniques and, 92,
  97–101

imaginal life, 71–76
 benefits of, 72
 development of, 85
 impact of affluence on, 123–24
 memories and, 73–76
 real world vs., 72–73
 stories and, 124

imitation, 68–69

Inconvenient Truth, An (film),
 168–69

India, ancient, 183–84

inner resources, 103

Institute of Cultural Affairs, 104

interconnectedness, 86–90, 172–73

Internet, 15

intuition, 97, 191

Inuit people, 188–89

Istanbul (Turkey), 122

J

Japan, 121

Jayne, David, 53

journey rides, 136–41, 143–47
Journey Ride to Your Heart's
    Desire (exercise), 143–47
Julie (author's friend), 69
Jumping Mouse parable, 112–13
Jung, Carl, 107, 142–43

K

Kate (author's friend), 87–90, 155
Kester, Denise, 117–19
Kohanov, Linda, 171–72
Koran, 44
Kysis (Arabian mare), 87

L

Labyrinth Project, 114
labyrinths, 113–16, 162
Lapdron, Machig, 35
leadership
    aggression vs., 48
    assertiveness and, 48, 49–50
    in human/horse partner-
        ships, 46, 47–52, 68–70
Lean on Me (exercise), 57–60, 153
Lebh Shomea House of Prayer
    (Sarita, TX), 121
Listening to Your Body (commu-
    nication exercise), 65–67, 153
Llewellyn, Morgan, 94–97
Long Soldier, Tilda, 166, 167
Lord of the Rings, The (film
    trilogy), 1, 18, 90
    allies in, 20
    guardians in, 20
    tests in, 21, 123

M

Macy, Joanna, 172
Madison (mare), 51–52, 61
Man and His Symbols (Jung), 107
mandalas
    labyrinths, 113–16
    Native American, 110–13
    Tibetan Buddhist, 113
Man Who Listens to Horses, The
    (Roberts), 30–31
Markale, Jean, 92–93
martial arts, 90
Mary (author's friend), 104–5
mask making, 173
McGehey, Kari, 154–55
Mead, Margaret, 169
Medicine Cards (Sams and
    Carson), 124–25
medicine wheel, xix, 110–13
medicine women, 166–67
meditation
    mindfulness, 150–51
    sitting, 150
    walking, 151–52, 156–57
Meeting Your Higher Self
    (exercise), 82–84
memory, 73–76
men
    competition and, 32
    hero's journey and, 26–27
    human/horse partnerships
        and, 30–31

mental health, therapeutic riding
and, 3–4, 105–6
Millionth Circle Initiative, 169–70
mimesis, 68–69
mind/body balance
labyrinths and, 114
sacred theater and, 141–43
mindfulness
exercise for, 156–57
with horses, 152–55
return with boon and, 150,
157
traditional practice of, 150
walking meditation, 151–52,
156–57
Minnesota Linking Individuals,
Nature, and Critters, 153
modern life. *See* everyday life
morphic fields, 170–72
motherhood, as hero's journey,
27–28
Murray, William Hutchinson, 20
music, 173
mysticism, 159–60
See also spiritual experiences
myth
archetypes and, 12–13
current crumbling of, 14
as foundational aspect of
self, 4, 8–9, 15–16, 73
future, 14–15
horses in, 9–11
humans and, 12–15
mythic life

human/horse partnerships
and, 176
as sacred theater, 131–32, 147
Mythology of Horses, The (Hausman and Hausman) circum-
flex, 108
"The Myth: Raison d'Être"
(Rogers), 9–10

N

National Center for Complementary and Alternative Medicine, 150
nationalism, 14
Native American cultures
drums in, 186–87, 188–89
feeding the demon in, 35–36
labyrinths derived from, 114
spiritual experience in,
165–67
symbols in, xix, 109–13, 120
natural world, connection with,
168–69, 172–73
Navajos, 110
New Feminine Brain, The
(Schultz), 26
North American Riding for the
Handicapped Association
(NARHA), xx, 2
nuclear bomb, as symbol, 107–8

O

Oglala Sioux, 109–10
Ojibwe, 186–87
oracles, 122

P

Painted Drum, The (Erdrich), 186–87
patriotism, 14
Pegasus, 11
Pictish art, 93
Plains Indians, 165–67
Praise Song from Violet Emerald, 178–79
Praise Song to Violet Emerald, 179
present moment, focus on, 150
primitive brain, 26–27
psychotherapy, 11–12, 150

Q

quantum nonlocality, 86–87
    See also interconnectedness
quantum physics, 86

R

Ramayana, xix
rationality, 97, 107
religion, 14, 107, 169
return
    everyday life and, 149–50
    in hero's journey, 18–19, 23–24
    mindfulness and, 150, 157
    See also boon, gaining of
Riding into a New Future (adventure game scenario), 41–42
Rig-Veda, 183–84
ritual
    in everyday life, 134–36
    in sacred theater, 133–34

    in therapeutic riding programs, 136–41
    transformative power of, 135–36, 141–43
    See also sacred theater
Roberts, Monty, 30–31
Rogers, Pattiann, 9–10
role-playing, 70
Rubin, Peggy Nash, 131–32, 188

S

sacred theater
    audience in, 138–39
    celebration as essence of, 133
    exercise for, 143–47
    healing power of, 141–43
    human/horse partnerships as, 132
    mythic life as, 131–32, 147
    ritual in, 133–34
    in therapeutic riding programs, 136–41
    See also ritual
safety, 55, 66
Sams, Jamie, 35–36, 124–25
sand paintings, 110–11, 113
Schultz, Mona Lisa, 26, 165
Seed, John, 172
self
    Chiron self, 143
    higher, meeting (exercise), 82–84
    levels of, 8
    mythic aspect of, 4, 8–9, 15–16, 73

self-doubt, 21

Senegal, 121, 122

Senior (lesson horse), 91–92

sensations, gender differences in, 30

senses, fine-tuning, 57–60, 103

Shandley, Melissa, 173

Sheldrake, Rupert, 87, 170–71

shield of power, 124–27, 137

Smith, Ara, 44–45

Social Artistry, 90–91

spiritual experiences
    author's, 160–65
    democratization of, 167–68
    global citizenship and, 168–69
    in Native American culture, 165–67
    social upheaval and, 159–60
    Western overlooking of, 165

Star Wars films, 18

Statue of Liberty, 13

stories
    conscious awareness of, 164–65
    healing through, 182–85
    horses in, 7–8
    mythic aspect of, 15–16, 123–24, 165
    symbols and, 123–24

Storm, Hyemeyohsts, 112–13

St. Pierre, Mark, 166, 167

strengths, 126

sun dance, 109–10

symbols

    animals as, 116–23
    commercial, 107
    Earth as, 107–8
    exercise for, 124–27
    harnessing power of, 106–9
    horses as, 104–6, 109–10, 117–19
    horseshoes, 108–9
    importance of, 103–4, 127–28
    labyrinths, 113–16
    mandalas, 110–16
    modern life and, 123–24

T

talents, 126

Tao of Equus, The (Kohanov), 171–72

TeachingHorse programs (Rogue River, OR), 114–16

teaching-learning communities, 169–70

telepathy, 170

Tellington-Jones, Linda, 97, 114

Tellington TTouch, 97–101

Terry (horse trainer), xiv–xvii

tests. *See* trials/adventures

theater, traditional, 131–32
    See also sacred theater

therapeutic riding programs, 2–4
    author's program, xix–xxi, 161, 164
    beginning of, 2
    growth of, 3–4

therapeutic riding programs
  (*continued*)
    mental health aspects of,
      3–4, 105–6
    professionalization of, 2–3
    sacred theater as used in,
      136–41
threshold crossing, 20–21, 133
Tibetan Buddhism, 113
Timmons, Tom, 180
touch techniques, 91–92, 97–101,
  103
transformation
    horses and, 2, 122–23
    symbols as key to, 104
treatment, as hero's journey, 24–25
trials/adventures, 113
    in hero's journey, 18, 21–22
    symbols needed for, 123–24
TTouch, 97–101
Turkey, 121–22
turtles, as symbols, 119–23

U

Ulysses, 18, 21, 123
Upanishads, 56

V

Valley of the Horses, The (Auel),
  62–65
Vibrational Medicine (Gerber), 91
violence, 174
visions, 161–64
voice signals, 68

W

Walking into Mindfulness
  (exercise), 156–57
Welsch, Tanya, 152–53
Widening Your World (exercise),
  174–76
wild horses, 109–10
Wild Horse Sanctuary (Hot
  Springs, SD), 109–10
Wilkinson, Patricia, 139–40
women
    assertiveness and, 48
    competition and, 31–32
    as healers, 166–67
    hero's journey and, 26–29
    human/horse partnerships
      and, 29
Women Who Run with the Wolves
  (Estés), 12
wounded healer archetype,
  142–43
writer's block, rituals for over-
  coming, 134–35

Y

yoga, 90
Your Shield of Power (exercise),
  124–27

Z

Zeus (thoroughbred), 154–55

ABOUT THE AUTHOR

A CERTIFIED THERAPEUTIC RIDING INSTRUCTOR, Patricia (Trish) Broersma founded and directed the Saddle Light Center, a nonprofit therapeutic riding program in San Antonio, Texas. She went on to re-establish, direct, and act as head instructor for HOPE Equestrian Center in Ashland, Oregon. She has been a certified instructor with North American Riding for the Handicapped (NARHA) since 1997. In fall 2007, she begins her term as president of the Equine Facilitated Mental Health Association, a section of NARHA that promotes standards of safety and professionalism in educational and mental health activities with horses.

Trish holds a master's in English from the University of Michigan and has been a licensed massage therapist in Oregon. Her writing has appeared in *Practical Horseman* and other publications. She has worked with Jean Houston as a staff member in Houston's multicultural human development work since 1990. She lives in Ashland, Oregon, and has three grown children.